ce

WILTSHIRE

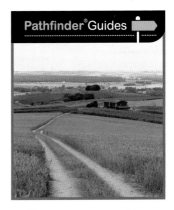

Pathfinder® Guides

Outstanding
Circular Walks

Compiled by
Dennis and Jan Kelsall

Contents

At-a-glance

Walk		Page	🗺		🏁	⛰	🕐
1	Downton and the River Avon	10	Downton	SU 175 214	4 miles (6.4km)	130ft (40m)	1¾ hrs
2	Marden Henge	12	Marden Village Hall	SU 085 577	4¼ miles (6.8km)	120ft (35m)	2 hrs
3	Old and New Wardour Castles	14	Old Wardour Castle	ST 938 264	4 miles (6.4km)	465ft (140m)	2 hrs
4	Devizes and Caen Hill Locks	16	Devizes, the Wharf Centre	SU 004 617	4¼ miles (6.8km)	230ft (70m)	2 hrs
5	Westbury White Horse and Combe Bottom	18	Bratton Camp	ST 899 513	4 miles (6.8km)	590ft (180m)	2¼ hrs
6	Lockeridge and Wansdyke	20	West Woods car park	SU 162 666	4½ miles (7.2km)	525ft (160m)	2¼ hrs
7	Fovant Down	22	Fovant, by the church	ST 996 295	4¾ miles (7.6km)	575ft (175m)	2½ hrs
8	Roundway Down	24	Roundway Hill Covert	SU 004 647	5 miles (8km)	695ft (210m)	2½ hrs
9	Broughton Gifford and Great Chalfield	26	Broughton Gifford Common	ST 874 641	5¼ miles (8.4km)	180ft (55m)	2½ hrs
10	Broad Chalke and the Ox Drove	28	Village car park, Broad Chalke	SU 040 254	5½ miles (8.9km)	460ft (140m)	2¾ hrs
11	Salisbury and Old Sarum	30	Salisbury	SU 143 300	5¾ miles (9.3km)	345ft (105m)	2¾ hrs
12	White Sheet Hill	34	The Clock Tower, Mere	ST 812 323	6 miles (9.7km)	690ft (210m)	3 hrs
13	Battlesbury, Midddle and Scratchbury Hills	37	Bishopstrow Church	ST 894 437	6¼ miles (10.1km)	785ft (240m)	3¼ hrs
14	Stourton and Alfred's Tower	40	NT car park, Stourhead	ST 779 340	6¼ miles (10.1km)	885ft (270m)	3¼ hrs
15	Pewsey Downs	43	Walkers Hill	SU 115 638	6¾ miles (10.9km)	740ft (225m)	3½ hrs
16	Bradford-on-Avon, Westwood and Avoncliff	46	Bradford-on-Avon	ST 826 608	7 miles (11.3km)	605ft (185m)	3½ hrs
17	Lacock and Bowden Park	50	Lacock, edge of the village	ST 918 682	7 miles (11.3km)	690ft (210m)	3½ hrs
18	Ludgershall Castle	53	Village car park	SU 264 508	7¼ miles (11.7km)	640ft (195m)	3½ hrs
19	Avebury, West Kennett and Silbury Hill	56	Avebury	SU 099 696	7½ miles (12.1km)	460ft (140m)	3½ hrs
20	Tollard Royal and Win Green	59	Tollard Royal	ST 944 178	6¾ miles (10.9km)	970ft (295m)	3½ hrs
21	Stonehenge	62	Amesbury	SU 149 411	7¾ miles (12.5km)	575ft (175m)	3¾ hrs
22	Great Bedwyn and Crofton Locks	65	Great Bedwyn	SU 280 644	8 miles (12.9km)	445ft (135m)	3¾ hrs
23	Martinsell Hill and the Kennet & Avon Canal	69	Martinsell Hill	SU 183 645	8 miles (12.9km)	655ft (200m)	4 hrs
24	Castle Combe	74	Upper Castle Combe	ST 845 777	8½ miles (13.7km)	850ft (260m)	4¼ hrs
25	Barbury Castle and Ogbourne St Andrew	77	Barbury Castle Country Park	SU 156 760	9 miles (14.5km)	755ft (230m)	4½ hrs
26	Savernake Forest	80	Marlborough	SU 188 692	8¾ miles (14.1km)	705ft (215m)	4½ hrs
27	Cherhill White Horse and Windmill Hill	84	A4 ¾m W of Beckhampton	SU 076 692	9¼ miles (14.9km)	855ft (260m)	4¾ hrs
28	Cold Kitchen Hill and Shear Water	88	Shear Water car park	ST 854 420	10 miles (16.1km)	1,100ft (335m)	5 hrs

Comments

An attractive village with unusual associations and splendid flower-rich water meadows and hedgerows are among the features of this short but enjoyable wander.

A gentle walk round the source waters of the western branch of the Hampshire Avon, finishing past a large prehistoric henge and a grand country pub.

This is a fine walk through landscaped parkland and woodland that links a ruined medieval castle with its 18th-century successor.

Whether or not you are a canal enthusiast, there is much of interest at the Wharf Centre in Devizes and when descending the Caen Hill flight of locks.

Wiltshire's oldest white horse, an early British fort and a Neolithic burial mound are among the sights on this walk that wanders between the tops and bottoms of Bratton Down.

Wansdyke, an important native British defence that ran for some 35 miles (56km) across the county, and a sarsen 'field' are two features of this pleasant woodland ramble.

Fovant churchyard and the regimental badges carved on the side of Fovant Down are reminders of the 1914–18 war. There are fine views from the top of the down.

The occasional strenuous sections of this walk are more than compensated by the superb views from the Iron Age defence of Oliver's Castle.

The National Trust's moated Great Chalfield Manor occupies a charming setting overlooking an ancient agricultural landscape of ridge and furrow fields and open village commons.

Wonderful views, flower-rich hedgerows and meadows, and a hilltop stretch along an ancient drove road are among the highlights of this walk.

A fascinating historic walk, much of it beside the River Avon, linking Salisbury with its now deserted predecessor.

Tucked below the steep escarpments of the downs, attractive Mere makes an excellent starting point for this exhilarating foray onto the high ground.

A stunning walk on the downs in an area particularly rich in chalkland wildflowers and the butterflies they attract. Keep your eyes open too for kestrels.

A grand walk linking the fine house, gardens and parkland of Stourhead with Alfred's Tower, an unusual monument visible for miles around.

You enjoy some fine downland walking, grand views over the Vale of Pewsey, two ancient churches and an attractive stretch of the Kennet and Avon Canal.

There are several hilly sections, but in between much pleasant and relaxing walking by the rivers Avon and Frome and the Kennet and Avon Canal.

An attractive route from charming Lacock, with superb views over the Avon Valley and the chance to explore a picturesque village and visit an interesting country house.

Once the playground of royalty, Ludgershall and its nearby forest offer endless opportunities for walks, while its castle ruin is worth a visit in its own right.

A fascinating walk on the Marlborough Downs, taking in the finest collection of prehistoric monuments in the country.

There are superb and extensive views both from Win Green, the highest point on Cranborne Chase, and the subsequent ridge top path.

The most memorable part of this thoroughly absorbing walk is the approach to Stonehenge across the wide expanses of Salisbury Plain.

There is plenty to see in the woods and parkland of the Tottenham estate and along a section of the Kennet & Avon Canal, as it drops from its summit pound past Crofton Pumping Station.

An enjoyable ramble offering great views from the edge of the down on Martinsell Hill, an easy stretch beside the Kennet & Avon Canal, and thatched cottages and a village pub in Wootton Rivers.

Castle Combe is one of the most picturesque villages in the area, and serves as the base for this splendid walk that combines delightful wooded valleys with rolling upland fields.

From an Iron Age hillfort high up on the Marlborough Downs, the route follows the Ridgeway down into the valley below and then climbs back onto the downs.

Most of this lengthy but rewarding walk is through the woodlands and along the grand beech-lined avenues of a former royal forest.

A grand circuit linking two of the area's fine viewpoints, with a white horse and prominent hilltop monument thrown in for good measure.

The heights of Cold Kitchen Hill and Whitecliff Down give expansive views, complementing a pleasant section through Longleat Forest and by the popular Shear Water.

Keymap

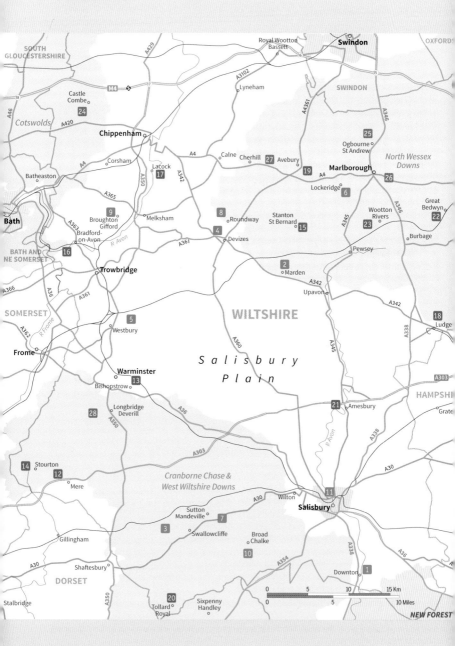

Introduction to Wiltshire

Set within the heartland of southern England, Wiltshire takes its name from Wilton, a once thriving Saxon town that grew around an 8th-century abbey. But with the founding of a cathedral and castle at nearby Old Sarum in the 11th century, it lost its primacy. However, Old Sarum came and went too, abandoned in 1220 after the bishop decided to move into the valley below to found New Sarum on the banks of the Avon, today known as Salisbury. Funded by a bounteous wealth derived from wool and the cloth trades, this was a purpose-built city with a new cathedral, which was constructed in less than 40 years and boasts the tallest spire in Britain.

Largely rural, Wiltshire has only one city and a handful of towns. These include attractive market towns that have retained their historic character and are a delight to explore, such as Malmesbury, Bradford-on-Avon and Devizes, which, incidentally, boasts the largest market square in the region and is home to the Wiltshire Museum, where half a million years of the county's history are showcased. Elsewhere, the population is centred upon small villages, among which are Castle Combe, Lacock and Tisbury, some of the prettiest villages in the country. Plentifully scattered across this expansive landscape are ancient castles, stately homes, village churches, grand abbeys and a fine cathedral.

But perhaps more than anything, Wiltshire is known for its fabulous wealth of prehistoric remains, a list that spectacularly includes Avebury, West Kennett, Silbury Hill, Windmill Hill and, of course, Stonehenge. In addition to these are countless lesser barrows, tumuli, earthworks, hillforts and trackways that together indicate the presence of sophisticated and highly organised communities stretching back through the Iron and Bronze ages to Neolithic times, the earliest finds being dated to around 8000BC.

It is a land where history, myth and legend have become inseparably linked. Liddington Castle north of Marlborough is one of the places put forward as the site of the Battle of Mons Badonicus, in which King Arthur led the native British against the Saxons, bringing a period of relative peace to the land. To the south lies Amesbury, regarded as the oldest known occupied settlement in Britain, where his queen found seclusion in the abbey convent following his death. Three hundred years later, Wiltshire lay on the northern border of Alfred the Great's kingdom of Wessex, and was where he in turn held back the Great Heathen Army of Danes at the Battle of Edington. Alfred had mustered his army on the hill above Stourton, where now stands Alfred's Tower. The land of Wessex lives on, given new life in the 19th-century novels of Thomas Hardy. And although much of the action is centred upon thinly disguised villages and landmarks in Dorset, Stonehenge is one of the places that has retained its identity and was chosen as the setting for the tragic climax of his *Tess of the D'Urbervilles*.

Dominating much of the landscape, and a wonderful draw for walkers, are the rolling chalk downs, part of a much larger swathe outcropping from Dorset eastwards and northwards to the Yorkshire Wolds, to East Anglia and the North and South Downs. Although much of this land is farmed, the steep escarpments and many of the tops are left as grazing grassland, which abounds in delicate wildflowers and attracts countless butterflies, bees and other insects. The scarps have also provided a gigantic scratchboard for artists, who have cut away the turf to create white horses. Today, Wiltshire has eight of them, the oldest dating back to 1778, as well as a number of military badges, cut on Fovant Down during the First World War. Commonwealth troops stationed in Wiltshire left their mark too; an Anzac symbol on Lamb Down at Codford and a Kiwi on the slopes of Beacon Hill above Bulford Camp.

Rising towards Battlesbury Hill

The largest single body of chalk upland lies at the heart of the county, Salisbury Plain, a vast plateau extending over some 300 square miles (780 square kilometres). It is here that Stonehenge occupies a low ridge in the centre of the plain. The monument is visible for miles around and surrounded by numerous other ancient sites. Since 1898, about half of the plain has gradually been taken over by the MoD to become the biggest military training area in the country. However, while on the one hand, large sections are inaccessible to the public, not being subject to modern farming practices and left largely undisturbed, it has become a haven for wildlife. Rare plants and invertebrates abound while the plain is recognised as an important breeding and wintering site for birds.

Elsewhere much of the chalk uplands lie within Areas of Outstanding Natural Beauty, protections that cover around 40 per cent of the county. The north-eastern corner lies within the North Wessex Downs AONB, and includes Savernake Forest and the Marlborough Downs, which has the greatest concentration of prehistoric remains in the country. Traversing the high ground is the

Standing stones at Avebury

Ridgeway, believed to be one of the oldest routeways in Europe and still bearing the tramp of feet today, being part of a long-distance National Trail that runs for 87 miles (139km) connecting Avebury to Ivinghoe Beacon, east of Aylesbury.

In the south of Wiltshire, straddling the borders with Hampshire and Dorset is the Cranborne Chase and West Wiltshire Downs AONB. This is a former hunting area and here the valleys that cut into the downs are more wooded. From the highest point on the chase at Win Green (911 feet, 277m) the views are magnificent and extend beyond the south coast to the Isle of Wight. The north western border of the county is a marked contrast because it fringes upon the Cotswolds, where the underlying stone is not chalk but oolite, a wonderful, golden-hued limestone that is incorporated in the delightful architecture of its towns and villages.

The hill country is broken by the broad valleys of Wiltshire's several rivers, and are equally worthy of exploration. Below the southern slope of the Marlborough Downs is the beautiful Vale of Pewsey, through which runs the Kennet and Avon Canal. It was built in the early 19th century to provide a waterway link between the great ports of London and Bristol, a route that was later followed by the railways. The rivers Wylye, Nadder, Bourne and Avon drain Salisbury Plain to the south.

There are few areas in the country where heritage and landscape are as closely interwoven and this collection of walks presents a glorious selection of the best Wiltshire has to offer. With a mixture of shorter and longer routes exploring the differing facets of its countryside, wildlife, and unique historical legacy, visiting old towns and idyllic villages, passing attractive pubs and appealing teashops, the area is full of fascinating places to seek out.

This book includes a list of waypoints alongside the description of the walk, so that you can enjoy the full benefits of gps should you wish to. For more information about route navigation, improving your map reading ability, walking with a GPS and for an introduction to basic map and compass techniques, read Pathfinder® Guide *Navigation Skills for Walkers* by outdoor writer Terry Marsh (ISBN 978-0-319-09175-3). This title is available in bookshops and online at os.uk/shop

Wildflower-filled verge along the track to Church Bottom from Broad Chalke

Start
Downton

Distance
4 miles (6.4km)

Height gain
130 feet (40m)

Approximate time
1¾ hours

Route terrain
Paths, tracks and lane

Parking
Car park behind Co-op off the village main street, B3080

OS maps
Landranger 184 (Salisbury & The Plain), Explorer 130 (Salisbury & Stonehenge)

GPS waypoints
- 📍 SU 175 214
- Ⓐ SU 180 215
- Ⓑ SU 182 222
- Ⓒ SU 182 234
- Ⓓ SU 176 236
- Ⓔ SU 174 222

Downton and the River Avon

This lovely walk winds through an interesting village to the outskirts of Trafalgar Park, gifted by the Government to the heirs of Admiral Lord Nelson in recognition of his services to the country. The return is by old flood meadows, created in the 17th century to provide lush summer grazing. They have become an important wildlife resource and remain vital in helping control winter floods along the River Avon.

📍 Return to the main road from the car park. **The Goat**, a possible port of call at the end of the walk, stands behind the old cross just to the left. However, to start the walk, go right through the attractive village. The road crosses three bridges over separate arms of the River Avon; the first a water management channel, the second the river itself, and the third a broad leat bringing water to the village's former mills. At one time there were over seven mills here by the river supporting a variety of industries including fulling, paper-making, grain production and tanning. One was even adapted to produce hydro-electricity. Although the industries have long gone, some of the buildings remain in the three houses below the bridge, while the large building on the left on the far bank was part of a tannery.

Turn off beside it along Church Leat Ⓐ, which leads into a small housing estate, developed on the site of the old tannery yards. Shortly, pass through a lychgate on the right into the large graveyard behind the Church of St Laurence. Head towards the church then bear right to exit by the southern lychgate. Go immediately left along a path past the Church Rooms, emerging beyond onto Barford Lane.

Follow it away to the left, leaving the village past Downton Cemetery and the Good Shepherd Catholic Church. Walk on for a further 300 yards before branching off left on a track towards Trafalgar Fisheries Ⓑ. Continue past the entrance to the trout farm, whose extensive pools lie either side of the main river channel, and on along a field track. Approaching a lodge cottage at the far end, look for a kissing-gate Ⓒ out of the field on the left. A path leads beside a high wall to emerge onto another track. Follow that left, past more buildings and the now redundant Standlynch Chapel, before swinging left to a bridge across a leat beside an old mill building.

The path turns right, crossing three more bridges before passing over the main river above a weir. The ongoing route meanders past reed beds, shortly crossing yet another bridge and stile that finally takes you back onto the

Weir and pathway bridge over the River Avon

Avon's west bank. Walk on over a bridged ditch and across a delightful water meadow beyond. Approaching trees and a pond, bear left on a fainter path. Leave the meadow at the far side through a kissing-gate onto the end of Warrens Lane by houses **D**.

Cross to another kissing-gate opposite and walk on by the right hedge. Keep ahead beyond its corner along the length of the field, maintaining the same line through hand-gates (faintly waymarked Avon Valley Path) across subsequent fields to end up walking alongside the left boundary. Emerge through a final kissing-gate onto a narrow lane and follow it ahead beside a tree-lined arm of the river.

Where the lane shortly bends round to the right **E** by New Court Farm, bear off left over an access bridge to a gate. A clear track, initially beside the water, runs on across another large water meadow, the ditches used for flood management being clearly visible. Through a gate at the far end, a path winds left to rejoin the river alongside the village's

modern flood defences. Coming out onto the main street, turn right back to the car park. ●

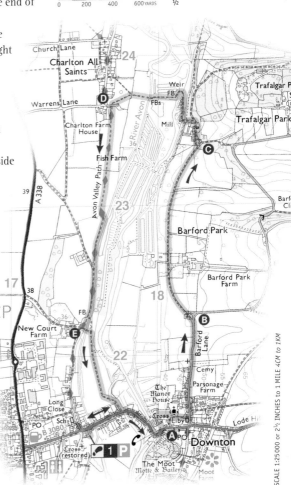

walk 2

Marden Henge

Start
Marden

Distance
4¼ miles (6.8km)

Height gain
120 feet (35m)

Approximate time
2 hours

Route terrain
Field paths and lane

Parking
Village hall car park

OS maps
Landranger 173
(Swindon & Devizes),
Explorer 130 (Salisbury
& Stonehenge)

GPS waypoints
- SU 085 577
- Ⓐ SU 073 575
- Ⓑ SU 075 581
- Ⓒ SU 080 583
- Ⓓ SU 083 589
- Ⓔ SU 086 591
- Ⓕ SU 092 588

Although much reduced by erosion and agriculture, Marden Henge, passed at the end of this delightful ramble, is nonetheless impressive for the area it covers. There are a couple of attractive village churches by the route and a lovely stretch alongside the watery meads bordering the upper reaches of the southern-flowing River Avon. But even here, there was enough water in the stream to drive a mill, which stood near the village's welcoming pub towards the end of the walk.

> **Marden Henge** Constructed some 4,500 years ago, the monument consisted of inner and outer henges and a massive barrow, or mound, said to have been 220 yards (200m) in diameter and 30 feet (9m) high. Excavation has discovered pottery, flints and animal bone, as well as the grave of a young female and there was also evidence of a wooden structure within the enclosure. The monument represents a huge investment of resources, but as with all such Neolithic sites, we can only guess as to their purpose.

Turn left out of the village hall car park and then take the first right. At the end, keep ahead through a farmyard to a stile and continue at the edge of a paddock. Emerging at a junction of tracks, take the grass path ahead, which finishes at the corner of another track. Follow it forward to come out onto the bend of a lane in Chirton. Walk ahead to the next bend Ⓐ and then turn off right into the churchyard. Walk round the west end of the church below the tower to leave the graveyard at the corner. A path to the right winds back to the lane. Follow it to the left.

Walking out of the village, look ahead-left to the distant hills where there is a view across the Vale of Pewsey to the Roundway White Horse. After ¼ mile (400m), just past a couple of cottages Ⓑ, leave to the right along a narrow lane. At a sharp bend, just before its end, turn off left and go through a small gate beside the entrance to a house. The path runs beside the building and over a bridge and stile into a meadow behind. Walk on at its right-hand perimeter, crossing out onto a path beyond. Ignore the small gate on the right and carry on ahead to cross a stile Ⓒ.

A grass path leads away to the right at the edge of wooded

wetland and waterside meadows. Winding round in a great loop, it eventually finishes through stock pens to emerge onto a lane at Limber Stone Bridge **D**. Go right towards Beechingstoke. Entering the hamlet, pass a row of houses on the right, at the end of which there is a footpath signed off beside them **E**. Follow it into the corner of a field and head away with the left boundary. Later, immediately

beyond a small wood, a waypost marks a path off right **F**.

Reaching a crossing track, walk ahead through a wide gap into the field opposite and bear left across it. Through a kissing-gate, continue in the next field, aiming left of a stable to find a stile behind. Maintain the same line across the corner of a final field to reach a lane. Although not overly obvious in the fields just crossed, Marden's henge can be better appreciated if you cross to follow the path in the field opposite.

Return to the lane and go left back to Marden, crossing the River Avon and passing **The Millstream** on your way back to the village hall. ●

SCALE 1:25 000 or 2½ INCHES to 1 MILE 4CM to 1KM

Cottage gardens at The Moors

Start

Old Wardour Castle, signposted from the A30 to the east of Shaftesbury

Distance

4 miles (6.4km)

Height gain

465 feet (140m)

Approximate time

2 hours

Route terrain

Pleasant paths, quiet country road, woodland and farmland tracks

P Parking

Old Wardour Castle

OS maps

Landranger 184 (Salisbury & The Plain), Explorer 118 (Shaftesbury & Cranborne Chase)

GPS waypoints

- ST 938 264
- **A** ST 934 261
- **B** ST 927 272
- **C** ST 931 276
- **D** ST 934 279
- **E** ST 941 271
- **F** ST 945 263

Old and New Wardour Castles

A ruined medieval castle and its 18th-century successor are linked by this undulating and interesting walk near the northern edge of Cranborne Chase. The route passes through a varied and attractive mixture of landscaped parkland, farmland and woodland. There is some modest climbing on the latter stages and a final descent through woodland.

The ruins of Old Wardour Castle are much enhanced by their romantic setting in landscaped grounds beside a lake and are well worth a visit. The hexagonal-shaped castle dates from the 14th century, but after its purchase by the Arundell family in 1570 it was partially rebuilt and made more comfortable. After the Civil War it was abandoned and fell into ruin but the landscaping of the grounds in the 18th century led to the building of a 'Gothick' summer house and the construction of a grotto, a popular contemporary feature.

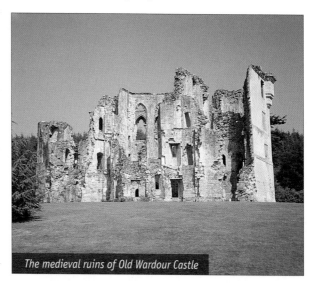

The medieval ruins of Old Wardour Castle

Start by taking the tarmac track that leads from the car park, passing between the castle on the left and the lake on the right. After passing to the right of the castle's 18th-century summer house, the track bends to the right and continues as a rough track. Later it becomes enclosed and keeps along the right inside edge of sloping woodland. To the right are grand views across the parkland.

By a waymarked post on the left, turn right **A** on to a clear track that curves left and heads gently downhill between wire fences. When the track bends sharp right, cross a stile on the left and continue towards the imposing bulk of the new Wardour Castle, a grand Georgian mansion built for the Arundells between 1770 and 1776. The house was sold after the Second World War and later used as a girls' school.

Climb a stile and continue ahead to pass in front of the house, curve right and pass between stone gateposts on to a lane **B**. Turn right and where the lane bends right, continue along the tarmac track to Bridzor Farm. Pass to the left of the farm and keep ahead, descending to a road **C**. Turn right, head uphill and at the top – just before a telephone box – turn right along a lane **D**.

Walk gently uphill along this tree-lined lane and keep along it for ³⁄₄ mile (1.2km) to where it bears right. At this point keep ahead **E** along a track, entering woodland. The track climbs quite steeply through the trees – at the top continue ahead as the track bends right to a house and continue along a grassy track. This is an area of mixed woodland, a most attractive part of the walk. At a junction of paths and tracks, turn right **F** along a track to emerge from the trees, and at an immediate crossroads keep ahead along an enclosed track across fields. The track then re-enters woodland and descends, passing under an arch, to the start. ●

SCALE 1:25000 or 2½ INCHES to 1 MILE 4CM to 1KM

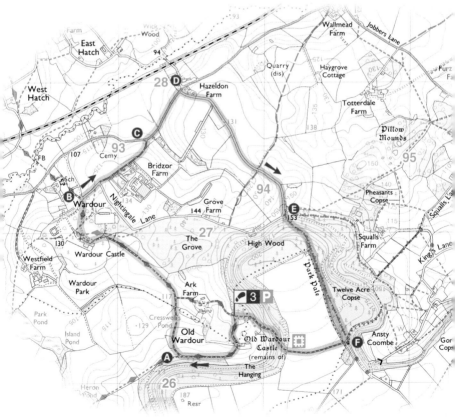

walk 4

Start
Devizes, the Wharf Centre

Distance
4¼ miles (6.8km)

Height gain
230 feet (70m)

Approximate time
2 hours

Route terrain
Easy towpath and tracks; some reasonably quiet road walking

P Parking
Wharf Centre, Pay and Display car park

OS maps
Landranger 173 (Swindon & Devizes), Explorers 156 (Chippenham & Bradford-on-Avon) and 157 (Marlborough & Savernake Forest)

GPS waypoints
SU 004 617
Ⓐ ST 993 615
Ⓑ ST 976 614
Ⓒ ST 979 619

Devizes and Caen Hill Locks

This is essentially a canalside walk and its main feature is the impressive Caen Hill Flight of locks, one of the major engineering triumphs of the canal age, by which the Kennet and Avon canal descends from the Vale of Pewsey to the Avon Valley. Canal lovers will find much of interest at the Wharf Centre in Devizes and there are fine views over the Avon Valley and downs.

The large, handsome Market Place is the main focal point of Devizes. The town boasts two medieval churches, both dating back to the 12th century; some fine Georgian houses; a Victorian brewery and a 19th-century castle built in the style of its Norman predecessor, on whose site it stands. By the canal, close to the town centre, is the attractively restored Wharf Centre. The two original buildings which survive now house a theatre and the headquarters of the Kennet and Avon Canal Trust – the latter, a former granary, has a shop and museum.

Facing the canal, turn right under the bridge, then sharp right up to the road and right again to cross the bridge. Turn left to walk along the canal towpath. Turn left over the first road bridge, left again at a public footpath sign 'Caen Hill Locks via Subway', and then turn sharp left to pass under the bridge.

Continue along the other bank of the canal, passing several locks, go under the next bridge (Prison Bridge) Ⓐ and keep ahead to reach the top of the Caen Hill Locks. This flight of 29 locks in just over 2 miles (3.2km) was built by John Rennie, the canal engineer, to overcome the problem of taking the canal up the 237 feet (72m) rise from the Avon Valley to Devizes. Sixteen of the locks were built close together down Caen Hill, a distance of only about ½ mile (800m).

As you descend gently beside these 16 locks there are fine views ahead over the Avon Valley. At the bottom of the flight

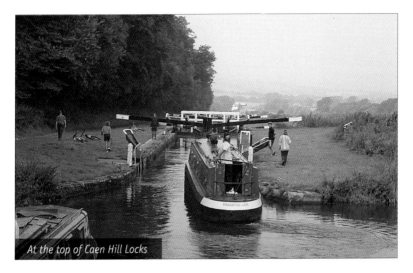

At the top of Caen Hill Locks

SCALE 1:25000 or 2½ INCHES to 1 MILE 4CM to 1KM

go under a bridge  B and immediately turn left up to a road. Turn sharp left to cross the bridge, continue along the road and at a sign for Caen Hill Locks, turn right along a tarmac lane **C**.

Follow the lane gently uphill. As it bears left, go right up steps. Turn left along a broad grassy swathe beside the

Side Pounds. These square-shaped ponds were built to provide a steady supply of water to the locks. Pass to the right of the parking area; keep ahead on a tarmac path. At the end of the grey metal fencing (right) keep ahead along a tree-lined track, to emerge onto a road. Turn right to cross Prison Bridge, turn left **A** and descend steps, then turn right on to the towpath and retrace your steps to the start.

0	200	400	600	800 METRES	1
KILOMETRES
MILES
0	200	400	600 YARDS	½

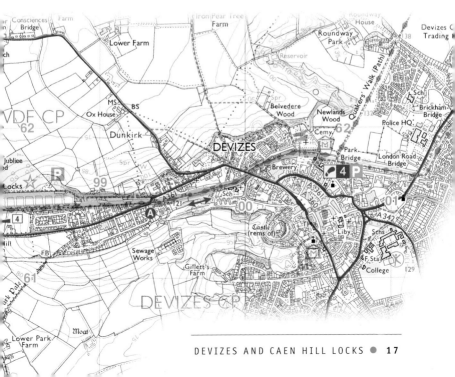

Start

White Horse car park,
Bratton Camp

Distance

4 miles (6.4km)

Height gain

590 feet (180m)

Approximate time

2¼ hours

Route terrain

Downland paths and
tracks, some lane

Parking

Large car park at start,
at the end of the Port
Way from Bratton
village

OS maps

Landranger 184
(Salisbury & The
Plain), Explorer 143
(Warminster &
Trowbridge)

GPS waypoints

ST 899 513
Ⓐ ST 900 511
Ⓑ ST 905 514
Ⓒ ST 914 519
Ⓓ ST 905 518

Westbury White Horse and Combe Bottom

*There have been 13 known white horses in Wiltshire, although
only eight remain clear today. Westbury's is the oldest and was
cut towards the end of the 17th century, perhaps to
commemorate the 9th-century Battle of Ethandun, when Alfred
the Great finally defeated the Danish hordes. The massive
figure, visible for miles around, lies on the hillside below
Bratton Camp, an impressive Iron Age stronghold. The walk
drops east from the hill for some splendid views across the
deep, dry valley of Combe Bottom to nearby Bratton, where
there is an interesting church and a pub.*

The best view of the Westbury White horse is to be had
from the edge of the escarpment opposite the car park. So begin
by crossing the lane from the western end of the parking area
to a kissing-gate. A path then continues out to the steep edge of
the hill, from which the horse can be seen over to the right.
Wander left round the rim, passing several seats which would
make ideal spots for a picnic at the end of the walk. There is
also a toposcope describing the view from this airy vantage.
Walk on round the edge for the view west and then head back
towards the car park.

Rejoining the byway, follow it left to a junction with the Port
Way (the lane onto the hill from Bratton) and go right. You can
avoid the tarmac by a parallel grass path running on the right.
The standing stone over to the right near the corner is a sarsen,
placed as a memorial to the Battle of Ethandun in 878. At the
end Ⓐ, go left past White Horse Farm along the Wessex
Ridgeway. After 600 yards, turn off left on a grassy bridleway
between the fields. Reaching a pair of gates, pass through the
left-most to continue with the track. A little farther on, at the
field corner, wind left and right and walk on to a crossway Ⓑ.
Go through a field gate and turn sharp right to a hand gate and
begin a lofty traverse above the deepening valley of Combe
Bottom. Through another gate, the path runs on by the right
fence, but watch for a waymark some 300 yards along
indicating a fainter path that branches down across the steep
slope, heading towards the church tower.

Nearing the field corner, ignore the bridle gate on the left and

Combe Bottom and St James's Church

carry on by the fence a little farther to a kissing-gate. Go through to reach another kissing-gate, but turn left in front of it beneath a giant sycamore and pick up a path that leads down to St James's Church **C**. Among its interesting features are a Norman font from the original church, intricate vaulting beneath the tower and a 19th-century painted sundial on the tower.

Head away from the church down a long flight of well graded steps into the bottom of the valley and continue up the other side, passing a lovely community orchard on your right. The path emerges onto a narrow lane at the edge of Bratton. For refreshment, turn up right into the village, bearing left at a tiny grass roundabout to find **The Duke at Bratton** on the main street.

Otherwise follow the narrow lane down to the left over a crossroads, signed to Bratton Castle. Beyond the last house, the way degrades to a track, coming out at the bottom onto a lane, the Port Way. Go left.

After 350 yards, leave the lane through a kissing-gate on the right **D**. Branch left, passing an abandoned livestock water tank bearing a painted smiley face and walk up between the outer ramparts of the Iron Age fort. Keep left as the path forks, paralleling the lane to then climb onto the main rampart of the Bratton Camp defences and follow it to the right. Continue round the perimeter, looking out over the impressive earthworks below. Turning the north-west corner brings you above the White Horse, but looking down on it from here gives a very distorted view. Stick with the defences as they head back towards the Port Way, although you might wander out left to look at the Neolithic long barrow, which predates the fort by some 3,000 years. Follow the defences round back to the Port Way and go right and right again back to the car park. ●

walk 6

Start
West Woods car park

Distance
4½ miles (7.2km)

Height gain
525 feet (160m)

Approximate time
2¼ hours

Route terrain
Woodland paths and lane

Parking
Car park at start, 1¼ miles (2km) south-east of Lockeridge

OS maps
Landranger 173 (Swindon & Devizes), Explorer 157 (Marlborough & Savernake Forest)

GPS waypoints
- SU 162 666
- Ⓐ SU 161 664
- Ⓑ SU 154 657
- Ⓒ SU 151 665
- Ⓓ SU 147 674
- Ⓔ SU 152 672
- Ⓕ SU 152 663

Lockeridge and Wansdyke

Although running through dense trees, the section of Wansdyke encountered on this largely woodland walk remains a striking monument, a deep outer ditch defending a high earth embankment. Farther along the route is an intriguing field of sarsen stones, while just up the road through the village is a pub, conveniently sited at the halfway point.

Leave the West Woods car park beside the barrier, where a path branches left off the main track into the trees. Coming to another broad forest trail, cross and continue with the rising path. It soon meets another forest trail Ⓐ by the corner of Wansdyke, a prominent embankment with a ditch in front, which can be seen in the trees opposite. Turn right.

Later, ignore a crossing path and carry on until you reach a broader one crossing on a slant. Go left through a break in the dyke, but then, after a few yards, branch off right to resume following the dyke on its inner flank. The trail eventually leads to a junction at the edge of the wood Ⓑ.

Double back right on a path heading north into the trees. It steadily falls for ¼ mile (400m) to meet the sharp bend of a forest road. Walk ahead on the descending branch, before long reaching a major junction. Go right, and at the next junction by a four-handed bridleway sign, turn left, soon reaching a fork by Forest Lodge Ⓒ.

Take the left branch up to a crossing path and walk right. The path gently gains height to the edge of the wood. Continue ahead beside the field boundary and then on along a path running within a strip of trees to emerge onto a road at the edge of Lockeridge Ⓓ. Turn right and immediately fork left into the village, passing a gate on the left into a small field littered with sarsens. Carry on with the lane into the village to find the curiously, but not uniquely named **Who'd A Thought It**.

Suitably refreshed, retrace steps through the village to a fork. Bear left and climb to the main lane. Cross to the narrow lane opposite and follow it up, passing the entrance to a farm at the top and round to the left to a car park at the northern edge of West Wood Ⓔ. Walk through and continue past a barrier at its far end. Keep with the main track as it bends right and carry on to a crossing, marked by a four-handed bridleway sign Ⓕ, seen earlier in the walk. Go left on a rising path, eventually emerging onto the bend of a forest road. Follow it ahead, back to the car park.

Wansdyke

SCALE 1:25000 or 2½ INCHES to 1 MILE 4CM to 1KM

Fovant Down

Start
Fovant, by the church at the north end of the village

Distance
4¾ miles (7.6km)

Height gain
575 feet (175m)

Approximate time
2½ hours

Route terrain
Near the start is a section of bridleway which can often be wet and muddy; downland paths and tracks. The last leg is by road through Fovant, back to the start

P Parking
By Fovant church

OS maps
Landranger 184 (Salisbury & The Plain), Explorer 118 (Shaftsbury & Cranborne Chase)

GPS waypoints
  ST 996 295
Ⓐ ST 998 291
Ⓑ SU 002 281
Ⓒ SU 005 274
Ⓓ SU 011 273
Ⓔ SU 019 279
Ⓕ SU 006 285

There are poignant memories of the First World War both at the start of the walk in Fovant churchyard and on Fovant Down, famed for its carvings of regimental badges. After an initial ascent and descent to the west of the village, a steady climb leads on to the crest of the down followed by a walk along the wooded ridge. The views from here are superb. The descent takes you across the face of the down past some of the badges, though these are best viewed from the bottom. The final part of the walk is through the attractive village of Fovant.

At the start of the walk you might like to enter the peaceful and attractive churchyard of Fovant's medieval church. Here are the graves of soldiers from all over the British Empire who died from injuries received during the First World War.

 Begin by walking back along the lane to a crossroads, turn left and at a public bridleway sign to the A30, turn right on to a tarmac track Ⓐ. After a few yards this becomes a grassy path, enclosed between hedges and trees, which heads gently uphill through a steep-sided valley to a fork and is often very muddy underfoot.

Continue along the right-hand enclosed path – this is narrow and likely to be overgrown – which descends gently to reach the A30 to the right of a farm Ⓑ. Cross over and take the lane ahead, signposted to Broad Chalke and Bowerchalke. Where the lane bends right in front of a chalk pit, bear left through a galvanised gate Ⓒ. Continue along the sunken path ahead, climbing steadily up to the ridge of the down, and head up through bushes to reach a gate beyond which is a crossroads Ⓓ. Turn left and walk along a broad, ridge top track through a narrow strip of wood-land. Open country can be glimpsed through the gaps in the hedgerow.

Where the track curves right, turn left over a stile Ⓔ and keep ahead along the right edge of the earthworks of Chiselbury Fort, an Iron Age hillfort which, at a height of 662 feet (201m), enjoys a commanding position and magnificent views. Shortly after following the curve of the fort gradually to the left, look out for a footpath sign on a fence on the right and head across.

Follow the path as it runs steeply and diagonally downhill, passing between more of the regimental badges, to the bottom corner of the down. Continue through bushes, keep ahead and go through a metal gate on the right. Walk along the left edge of a field to a metal gate in the corner. At this point look back for a good view of the Fovant Badges, a series of regimental badges carved on the side of the down by troops stationed here in the First World War.

Go through the gate and turn left along a straight, enclosed track, passing to the left of a large farmhouse. Later the track bears left, then turns right and continues between houses to emerge on to a lane on the edge of Fovant. Keep ahead through the village to the main road **F**, cross over and continue along the lane opposite through this long and strung out village. At a fork in front of the village hall take the left-hand lane, signposted to Tisbury, and at a crossroads turn right along Church Lane to return to the start. ●

SCALE 1:25000 or 2½ INCHES to 1 MILE 4CM to 1KM

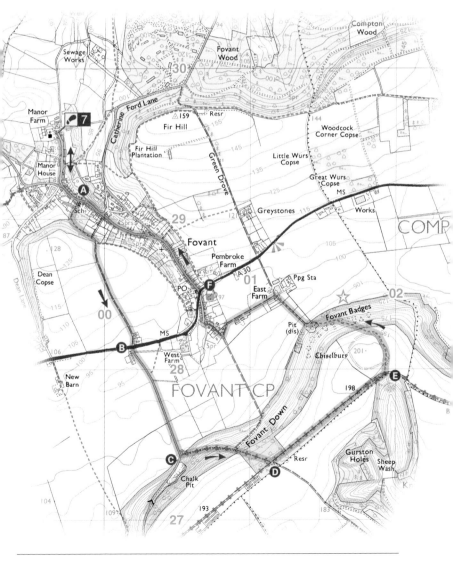

Roundway Down

Start

Roundway Hill Covert

Distance

5 miles (8km)

Height gain

695 feet (210m)

Approximate time

2½ hours

Route terrain

Tracks, field paths and lane

P Parking

Covert car park on Roundway Hill

OS maps

Landranger 173 (Swindon & Devizes), Explorers 156 (Chippenham & Bradford-on-Avon) and 157 (Marlborough & Savernake Forest)

GPS waypoints

SU 004 647
Ⓐ SU 007 639
Ⓑ SU 010 639
Ⓒ SU 012 633
Ⓓ SU 006 633
Ⓔ ST 996 650
Ⓕ ST 992 654
Ⓖ SU 000 646

Although not particularly long, this route includes a strenuous climb onto Beacon Hill towards the end of the walk, but the effort is amply repaid by the superb setting of Oliver's Castle, an impressive Iron Age hillfort strategically set above the lip of the escarpment. The walk begins through a woodland nature reserve before dropping off the hill, when there is a view back to one of Wiltshire's many white horses.

The Roundway White Horse

In the middle of the 19th century, there was a white horse – known as Snob's or Shoemakers' Horse – on the eastern slope below Oliver's Castle, but not being maintained it has all but disappeared. The one seen today, further east above Roundway Farm is a relative newcomer, and created in 1999 to celebrate the millennium.

A gate from the corner of the parking area leads into Roundway Hill Covert. Take the trail ahead and, where it shortly divides, keep with the left branch by the perimeter of the wood. Eventually coming to a T-junction, go left and carry on to a fork. The left branch leads you out to the corner of the wood Ⓐ.

Strike out across the width of a field to a track at the far side. Go right for 200 yards and then turn off through a kissing-gate on the right Ⓑ. Heading straight down the hill at the field edge, glance back up left for a view of the Roundway White Horse on the hillside. At the bottom, cross a field track to another kissing-gate, from which a path winds down through trees to emerge onto Consciences Lane Ⓒ.

Follow it down to the right for nearly ½ mile (800m) to find a path signed off beside a field gate on the right Ⓓ. Walk away by the hedge along the edge of a lengthy field at the foot of the steep slope of Roundway Hill. Keep going over a couple of fence boundaries, passing below Oliver's Castle. The field edge then curves uphill. Ignore a gate on the left part-way up and carry on to the top corner where there is a stile out onto a track Ⓔ.

Follow it left for ½ mile (800m). As the way then swings down left to meet the end of a broad track, watch for a path leaving into the bushes on the right Ⓕ. Turn up through scrub onto the open down and follow the path steadily up the steep flank of Beacon Hill. Through a fence higher up, keep going and eventually curve round to the right in front of a fence along the top boundary. Walk on into the corner where there is a gate. However, ignore it and turn right. Stay with the higher

Oliver's Castle The sparse stand of trees atop the stubby promontory of Roundway Down gives the hill a distinctive appearance that is recognisable for miles around. It is the site of an Iron Age fort, dating from around 600BC, one of several along the edge of the downs above the Vale of Pewsey. The one here is triangular in plan; two sides naturally protected by steep escarpments, while a substantial ditch and embankment across the neck of the promontory defend the third. It became known as Oliver's Castle after a Civil War battle here in 1643, when Parliamentarian forces, despite having the advantage of numbers and holding the high ground, were routed by Royalists, who had broken out from being besieged at Devizes. However, as Oliver Cromwell was elsewhere at the time, the place should perhaps have been named William's Castle after Sir William Waller, the Parliamentarian commander in the field.

path where it then forks, shortly passing through a gate. Continue round the rim of Oliver's Castle to the point of the promontory **G**.

Carry on round the edge above a deep valley. Keep going past a junction, eventually turning out through a kissing-gate. The car park is then just to the right.

SCALE 1:25000 or 2½ INCHES to 1 MILE 4CM to 1KM

Oliver's Castle

Broughton Gifford and Great Chalfield

Start

The Bell on The Common, Broughton Gifford

Distance

5¼ miles (8.4km)

Height gain

180 feet (55m)

Approximate time

2½ hours

Route terrain

Fields paths and lane

Parking

Roadside parking around The Common

OS maps

Landranger 173 (Swindon & Devizes), Explorer 156 (Chippenham & Bradford-on-Avon)

GPS waypoints

 ST 874 641
Ⓐ ST 865 644
Ⓑ ST 859 639
Ⓒ ST 860 632
Ⓓ ST 871 632
Ⓔ ST 877 637
Ⓕ ST 881 647
Ⓖ ST 874 647

Built for a wealthy 15th-century lawyer, Great Chalfield Manor has been wonderfully restored to reflect its former glory. The surrounding countryside reveals something of the medieval agricultural past in large, open commons and traces of ridge and furrow cultivation in what would previously have been open, communal fields. This contrasts with the latest innovation in land use, where fields are turned over to arrays of solar panels for the production of 'green' electricity.

 Begin facing **The Bell** and follow the lane left along the foot of The Common towards Great Chalfield and South Wraxall. Beyond the village, ignore the narrow lane signed to Great Chalfield, passed off left, and walk on for another 150 yards. Approaching a bend, cross to leave through a bridle gate on the left Ⓐ and walk away at the edge of a long field. Through gates, continue at the perimeter of another couple of fields to Lenton Farm.

Entering the farmyard, immediately turn right to leave through another gate. Walk forward and then swing left round a play area to skirt behind the farm buildings. Towards the far end, move right to a field gate by a stream Ⓑ. Through that, bear left across the corner to another gate and walk on by the winding left edge of the subsequent field. Through a gate, carry on, still beside the left hedge. Through a gap in the next corner, cross a stream and go left beside the field boundary. Passing into yet another field, turn right and follow the hedge towards a house beyond its far end. Leave at the corner into a final paddock and walk forward to a stile onto a track. Go left to emerge at the bend of a lane beside the entrance to the National Trust's Great Chalfield Manor Ⓒ.

Follow the lane ahead beside the moat with house and chapel behind. Approaching the next bend, turn off left beside a redundant stile and walk away at the perimeter of a large field. At the far end, go through a gap and over a bridged ditch onto the edge of pasture. Turn right by the hedge, but where the field narrows towards its end, move across to join the left boundary. Through a bridle gate in the corner, walk away by the right hedge, continuing in the subsequent field. Entering a third field Ⓓ, where the undulations of medieval ridge and furrow ploughing can still be seen, bear left with a footpath arrow to parallel the boundary. Keep ahead past an indent and clump of trees to a kissing-gate.

Head out on a right diagonal to a second kissing-gate and continue the line across the next field. Through another kissing-gate, ignore a crossing grass track and carry on, now heading towards a stone house. Cross a final paddock to come out in Broughton Gifford **E**.

Briefly follow the street right before turning left into Newleaze Park. Just round a bend, swing right into a short cul-de-sac. Leave through a gate at its end into the field behind. Head out to the far side, continuing across a small meadow and along a drive out to a lane. Climb a stile opposite, and strike out to a gate in the far-right corner. Go left and then keep ahead over a loose wire fence to carry on beside the left hedge. A kissing-gate in the corner leads onto the edge of a solar farm. Walk forward a few yards to find another kissing-gate on the left and head away by the right hedge. Towards the far end, look for a final kissing-gate on the right which opens onto a hedged track. To the left it takes you to the bend of a lane at the edge of Norrington Common.

Follow the lane ahead. After 200 yards, as it curves right onto the common, look for a sign indicating a footpath off left **F**. Walk past a small pond and fowl pens to find a stile in the hedge behind onto the perimeter track of another solar farm. Go forward to the corner, there passing through a gap into the next enclosure. Follow the grass swathe right, left and left again round the rows of solar panels to a gate, part-way along on the right. Slip through to continue on the other side of the hedge in the adjacent enclosure. Swing right within the corner and walk to the end, where a stile leads out to a farmyard **G**.

Cross the yard and leave along its access track. After some 60 yards, watch for a stile on the right; it gives access onto the top corner of the common. Head across to the lane at the far side and go left back to The Bell. ●

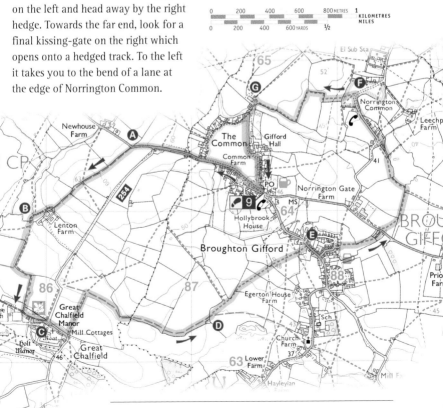

Broad Chalke and the Ox Drove

Start
Broad Chalke

Distance
5½ miles (8.9km)

Height gain
460 feet (140m)

Approximate time
2¾ hours

Route terrain
Downland paths, tracks and lane

Parking
Church and village hall car park by All Saints' Church

OS maps
Landranger 184 (Salisbury & The Plain), Explorer 130 (Salisbury & Stonehenge)

GPS waypoints
SU 040 254
Ⓐ SU 042 251
Ⓑ SU 052 229
Ⓒ SU 038 223
Ⓓ SU 035 230
Ⓔ SU 029 238
Ⓕ SU 033 248
Ⓖ SU 036 253

At the head of the River Ebble, Broad Chalke has grown around a cluster of crystal clear chalk springs, from which the village derives its name and have supported watercress farming for nearly 150 years. The walk begins along the dry valley of Church Bottom, climbing past a flower-rich nature reserve onto an ancient track running across the downs, from which there are splendid views across the surrounding countryside. Back in the village, at the other end of Causeway Bridge, there is a pub to relax in at the end of the day.

Leave the car park by the vehicle entrance and turn right along the lane. Almost immediately on your left is the Mill Mead Conservation Area. Reaching a junction, bear off left towards Martin and Blandford. At the next junction Ⓐ, cross to the track opposite, which leads past a group of houses. Beyond a barrier, pass a footpath signed off left and continue with the tree-lined track towards Church Bottom. Keep your eyes open for red kites soaring high above on thermals, while the verges and hedgerows on either side are full of chalk-downland flowers. As the valley later narrows, the track passes a group of stock pens and begins to climb beside the Middleton Down Nature Reserve, ultimately meeting a junction by the saddle of the down Ⓑ.

Turn right, now walking along the ancient Ox Drove. Ignore tracks leaving left and then later right to continue past barns and then Lodge Farm, which was once a remote drover's inn. Walk on a little further to meet a lane by Knowle Hill House Ⓒ.

Middleton Down Nature Reserve

Lying beside the path above Church Bottom, Middleton Down Nature Reserve begs exploration. Mainly consisting of open grassland, which is managed by grazing Dexter cattle, there are areas of wood and scrubland too. The open slopes support a wide variety of flowers such as vetches and trefoils and in spring and early summer you can find many species of orchid, including the common spotted, purple, pyramidal, fragrant, bee and frog, as well as autumn lady's-tresses later in the year. The flowers in turn attract bees, grasshoppers and butterflies like the rare Adonis blue. Come as the light fades on a late summer evening and you will likely spot glow worms, which are in fact beetles, the wingless females advertising their presence in the hope of attracting a mate.

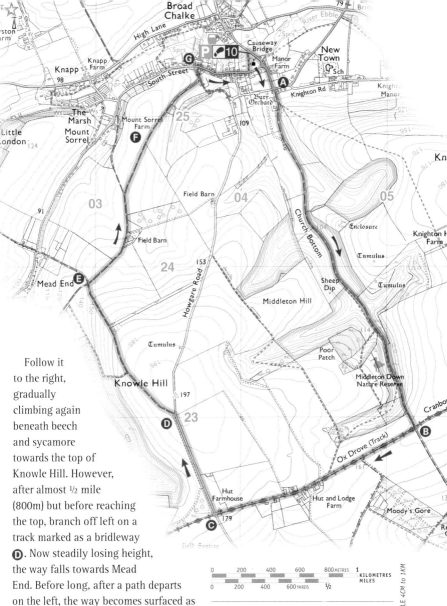

Follow it
to the right,
gradually
climbing again
beneath beech
and sycamore
towards the top of
Knowle Hill. However,
after almost ½ mile
(800m) but before reaching
the top, branch off left on a
track marked as a bridleway
D. Now steadily losing height,
the way falls towards Mead
End. Before long, after a path departs
on the left, the way becomes surfaced as
a narrow lane and descends for another
650 yards to a junction **E**.

Swing right and carry on down the
hill, shortly bending left past storage
containers at Field Barn. Keep left
beyond these and stick with the main
gravel track as it bends right further on,
soon reaching its end where it turns
into a field **F**. Continue with the
bridleway ahead, through a hand gate
along a delightful grass track.
Eventually, at a junction in front of a

thatched wall at the bottom, go left,
walking out to a lane in Broad Chalke
G. Turn right through the village past
attractive thatched cottages and
Reddish House, once the home of Sir
Cecil Beaton. Other one-time residents
of the village were Sir Terry Pratchet,
author of the Discworld novels and Sir
Anthony Eden, a former prime minister.
Reaching the village hall, take a
contained path off on the left, which
leads back to the car park. ●

walk 11

Salisbury and Old Sarum

Start

Salisbury

Distance

5¾ miles (9.3km)

Height gain

345 feet (105m)

Approximate time

2¾ hours

Route terrain

Leafy paths, pavements and riverbank

Parking

Pay and Display car parks in Salisbury

OS maps

Landranger 184 (Salisbury & The Plain), Explorer 130 (Salisbury & Stonehenge)

GPS waypoints

⬚ SU 143 300
🅐 SU 141 309
🅑 SU 128 320
🅒 SU 130 325
🅓 SU 133 327
🅔 SU 135 327
🅕 SU 140 326
🅖 SU 135 317

There is considerable historic interest on this walk linking New Sarum (or Salisbury) in the Avon Valley with Old Sarum, its predecessor, on the hill above. The first part of the route follows a delightful stretch of the River Avon to Stratford sub Castle before heading up to the remains of Old Sarum. From this hilltop position you enjoy extensive views over Salisbury, the Avon Valley and Salisbury Plain before descending to rejoin the river. Allow plenty of time to explore both the beautiful cathedral city of Salisbury and the remains of Old Sarum.

The cathedral and city of Salisbury were built on a new site when the seat of the bishop was moved there from Old Sarum in 1220. As a result Salisbury is a rare example of a planned medieval city, laid out on a grid system. Around the spacious Market Place and Guildhall Square, the heart of the city, much of the original street pattern and a number of fine medieval buildings survive.

Standing in a green, walled close – the largest in England – and lined with an assortment of distinguished buildings from the Middle Ages to the 18th century, Salisbury is the only medieval cathedral conceived and completed as a whole. It was built in a remarkably short time, between 1220 and 1258, and therefore has a unique uniformity of design. Only the upper part of the tower and spire came later, in the early 14th century. The cathedral is a supreme example of the Early English style, with an elaborate west front and lofty nave and choir. In such a spacious setting its beauty can be appreciated from all angles,

The ruins of the former glory of Old Sarum

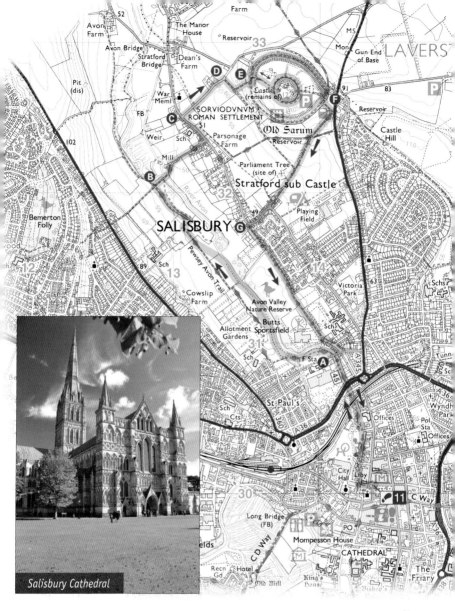

Salisbury Cathedral

but the undoubted crowning glory is the graceful, soaring spire, 404 feet (123m) high, the tallest in the country.

✎ The walk starts at the north-west corner of the Market Place. Cross Minster street into covered Market Walk, following signs to Riverside Walk, cross the River Avon and immediately turn right on to a tarmac path beside it. This is part of the Avon Valley Cycleway. Keep beside the river, passing to the right of car parks and going under several bridges and across roads, to reach a wooden bridge on the edge of parkland **A**.

From here continue along a gravel path beside the river, cross a bridge by a children's play area and immediately turn right to continue along a gravel path.

Take the right-hand – and main –

SCALE 1:25000 or 2½ INCHES to 1 MILE 4CM to 1KM

Old Sarum

Old Sarum is a fascinating place, for where else can you explore the site of an abandoned medieval city and, at the same time, look down on its successor? As early as the Iron Age a fort was established on this hilltop, but it was after the Norman Conquest that Old Sarum became a thriving city, with the headquarters of the diocese moving here in 1075, and the building of a castle. Several factors led to its decline – the combination of a cramped hilltop position, the lack of a water supply and quarrels between the cathedral and castle caused the bishop to move down the hill in 1220 and found New Sarum or Salisbury. What remains today within the vast earthworks of the outer defences are the bishops' palace, the Norman cathedral and the foundations and some of the walls of the castle, which occupies the centre of the site. As an added bonus, the views of the surrounding countryside are superb.

path, rejoining the Avon, and continue along a lovely, tree-lined stretch of the river. Mud can be a problem on these low lying riverside meadows and part of the route is across boardwalks. Where these end, keep ahead, go through a metal gate. Continue across the meadow and head away from the river. Continue on the path to a fence-gap, turn right along a path **B**, and cross a bridge over the Avon. Keep ahead, pass beside a metal barrier, soon merging onto a lane, and continue to a T-junction in Stratford sub Castle. Ahead is a fine view of Old Sarum.

Turn left along a road and just before it bears right by the church – medieval, but with a west tower that was rebuilt in 1711 – turn right on to an enclosed, tarmac path **C**. Follow the path uphill and as it bends to the left, look out for a tree-lined path on the right **D**.

Continue along this for 100 yards,

turn left through a wooden gate, and ascend the hill. Near the top bear left, climbing to a gate giving access to the steep ramparts. *To explore the castle remains, now managed by English Heritage, take the next path on the right* **E**. Otherwise, continue ahead through a gate and follow this exhilarating stretch along the outer ramparts of the castle. Go through a kissing-gate on to a tarmac drive **F**, which is the main entrance to Old Sarum.

Turn right, go through a small wooden gate ahead, and follow the path downhill. Go through another gate, continue downhill and a few yards before reaching a road, turn right on to a track, at a half-hidden green waymark. Continue by a hedge along the right edge of a field and halfway across turn left, aiming for a gap in the hedge. Turn right downhill on an enclosed path to eventually pass the Parliament Stone, by a kissing-gate on the right. Near here elections were held for the 'rotten borough' of Old Sarum, so called because, despite having only a handful of voters, it used to elect members to Parliament until such seats were abolished by the Great Reform Act of 1832.

Continue gently downhill and eventually the path broadens out into a track, which leads on to a road. Keep ahead and where the road bends right, turn left between posts **G**, at a public footpath sign to the City Centre, and walk along an enclosed path, between a hedge on the left and a wooden fence bordering a meadow on the right. Later keep ahead along a pleasant, tree-lined, tarmac track and where this ends, with the leisure centre on the right, bear right and cross the wooden bridge over the River Avon **A**, to rejoin the outward route.

Turn left beside the river and retrace your steps to the start. ●

King Alfred's Tower

White Sheet Hill

🖊 Start
The Clock Tower, Mere

🏁 Distance
6 miles (9.7km)

⛰ Height gain
690 feet (210m)

🕐 Approximate time
3 hours

🥾 Route terrain
Downland paths and tracks, some lane

P Parking
Pay and Display car parks in Castle Street and Salisbury Street in Mere

🗺 OS maps
Landranger 183 (Yeovil & Frome), Explorers 142 (Shepton Mallet & Mendip Hills East) and 143 (Warminster & Trowbridge)

📍 GPS waypoints
🖊 ST 812 323
Ⓐ ST 808 330
Ⓑ ST 805 347
Ⓒ ST 804 347
Ⓓ ST 797 349
Ⓔ ST 788 346
Ⓕ ST 802 327
Ⓖ ST 809 325

The historic small town of Mere, an interesting place in its own right, is the start of this exhilarating walk onto White Sheet Hill, where there is an extensive complex of Iron Age defences and dykes. The views into the natural amphitheatre of Great Bottom are spectacular, as it climbs along a narrow chalk ridge onto the hill, the high point providing a grand panorama across Stourhead to King Alfred's Tower. The grand finale is onto the impressive mound of Castle Hill, which, like Zeals Knoll, is isolated from the main run of the down.

🖊 Begin from the Clock Tower by **The George Inn** in the centre of Mere (turn right out of Castle Street car park or left from Salisbury Street car park). Cross to Manor Road opposite, past an antiques shop (right), and follow it out of town and over the bypass. Just after passing Manor Farm, turn off through a gate on the right along a track signed as a bridleway Ⓐ. Then, where it shortly bends right, keep ahead on a farm track rising onto the down, waymarked the Mid Wilts Way. Swinging left higher up through a couple of field gates, it continues to climb along a narrow ridge, from which there is an impressive view across Great Bottom to the right. Out to the west is King Alfred's Tower, which is visited on Walk 14.

Keep going as another track joins from the left, but then watch for a path forking off left through a field gate a little higher up. It curves away with a fence on the left round the edge of the escarpment. Reaching the corner of a covered reservoir enclosure Ⓑ, branch off right across the open field, making for a gate at the far side in front of stock pens. Emerging onto a track, go left, soon merging with a service track from the reservoir compound. Carry on just a little further to find a stile and then a gate on your left, through which walk onto the hillside. Wander back left to the summit of White Sheet Hill Ⓒ, which is marked by a trig column and surrounded by the prominent embankment defences of a prehistoric hillfort, White Sheet Castle. Today the hillside is a popular spot for model glider enthusiasts.

Return across the down, picking up a path above the escarpment rim; it later curves left and descends to a small car park Ⓓ. There, another path leaves in the opposite corner, passing through a gate to continue at the perimeter of a field.

Heading back to Castle Hill

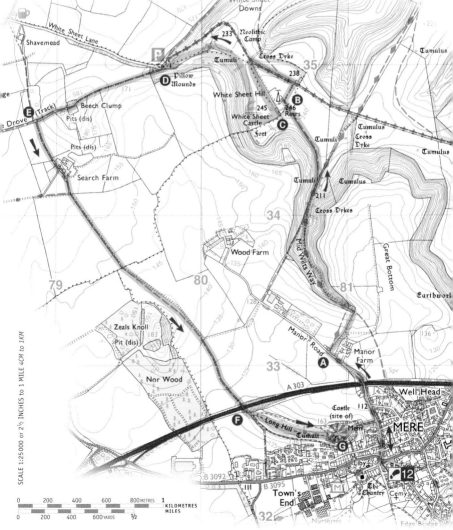

SCALE 1:25000 or 2½ INCHES to 1 MILE 4CM to 1KM

Mere Castle Although the mound and earthworks on Castle Hill overlooking the town remain a formidable sight, the castle was abandoned during the 14th century and dismantled. The lead roofs and fittings were reused during the refortification of Portchester Castle while the rest served as a ready-cut stone quarry for the developing town, which prospered on the back of a booming wool and linen trade and thriving market. The castle had been built in 1253 by Henry III's brother, Richard Earl of Cornwall; rectangular walls protected by six towers contained a main hall and chapel. It was later gifted to Piers Gaveston, whose overly close relationship with Edward II ultimately led to his downfall and execution in 1312. The castle subsequently reverted to the crown but was no longer used.

Walk on in the next field towards a stand of trees, Beech Clump, where there is a poignant memorial. It remembers 20 crew and servicemen killed when a Dakota crashed in 1945 shortly after leaving RAF Zeals en-route for its base at Leicester East. The plane failed to gain enough height after take-off and, in poor visibility, crashed into the clump of trees.

Continue along the ongoing track for another 250 yards before turning off left along a field-edge track **E** towards Search Farm. Pass the front of the farm and walk forward to join its access drive, but as that swings left into the yard, keep ahead on a stony track past a cottage. Reaching a junction with the fields ahead, go left and then right to stride on at the edge of a larger field with the hedge on the right. Entering the next field, walk forward with the boundary now on the left, passing Zeals Knoll over to the right. A little farther down, wind past a gap into the adjacent enclosure and continue with the hedge

still on the left, shortly crossing a bridge back over the Mere bypass **F**.

Wind left and then right to a kissing-gate at the foot of Long Hill. Climb steeply to the ridge top, gently dropping beyond the summit past a memorial to a kissing-gate. Keep ahead to climb the steps onto the top of Castle Hill **G**, and this is well rewarded for the expansive views. Return down the stairs off the castle mound and contour round left to go down two more flights of steps, leaving the hill past an information board. Through a kissing-gate, walk along an enclosed path past a playground and across a lane to continue down the alley opposite, coming out onto Castle Street. The clock tower is to the left but, if you have time before leaving, wander round the town. There is a small museum on Barton Lane and St Michael's Church has several interesting features. ●

Clock Tower, Mere

Battlesbury, Middle and Scratchbury Hills

walk 13

Connected by low saddles and separated from the main mass of Salisbury Plain by a deep, dry valley, the three hills to the east of Warminster above the Wylye valley present an exciting prospect for a walk. Each has well-defined and interesting earthworks, burials and cultivation patterns, and gives stunning views across the surrounding countryside.

From the end of the lane facing the church, turn left. Where the track peters out, keep ahead through a metal gate and follow the ongoing path, eventually crossing a bridge over the River Wylye to come out onto a road at the edge of Woodcock. Cross and follow the footway left for 100 yards before taking a driveway off on the right **Ⓐ** to Home Farm. Beyond Bishopstrow Court, pass beside a gate as the tarmac gives way to gravel. At the end of the track, wind left and then right to pick up a path that shortly goes over a bridge spanning the railway. It is hard to ignore the crossing concrete track just a little further along, but do, and continue towards the high ground ahead along a broad grassy way, the gradient gradually increasing. Over to the left, the hillside is terraced in strip lynchets, the result of centuries of ancient ploughing, while to the right the ground rises to Middle Hill, visited later in the walk.

Keep going until the grass swathe ends before a crop field and a four-way sign over to the right marking a crossing path **Ⓑ**. Go left beside the crop, climbing onto Battlesbury Hill. Towards the top, pass through a kissing-gate onto the ramparts of the hillfort and follow a path that takes you round the perimeter of the site. The multiple lines of the defences make full advantage of the topography and are particularly impressive on the northern flank. There are splendid panoramic views in all directions and a great vantage across the MOD training ranges to the north and east.

Return to the kissing-gate and descend along the outward path. There is now a grand view ahead to Middle Hill, where there are more impressive lynchet terraces on the northern slopes. Back at **Ⓑ**, this time keep ahead, making for the lynchet

---

Sidebar

Start
St Aldhelm's Church, Bishopstrow; alternative start below Scratchbury Hill at **Ⓒ**

Distance
6¼ miles (10.1km)

Height gain
785 feet (240m)

Approximate time
3¼ hours

Route terrain
Downland paths and tracks, some lane

Parking
Considerate parking along lane to church (particularly Sunday mornings and cricket match days) or small car park below Scratchbury Hill **Ⓒ**

OS maps
Landranger 184 (Salisbury & The Plain), Explorer 143 (Warminster & Trowbridge)

GPS waypoints
- ST 894 437
- **Ⓐ** ST 894 441
- **Ⓑ** ST 904 455
- **Ⓒ** ST 910 446
- **Ⓓ** ST 899 439

Middle and Scratchbury Hills from Battlesbury Hill

terraces. At the end of the field, step out onto a wide lane.

Go right, but then after a few yards, leave through a gap in the left bank, which gives access onto the down behind. Ignore the tyre tracks ahead and instead strike out diagonally to the right of them on a single grass trod. As you climb across the slope, a signpost shortly appears ahead at the corner of a fence. As the Right of Way avoids the summit, you should carry on beside the fence on your right round the western slope of the hill until you reach another signpost. The path then delves through a belt of trees to emerge lower down. A clear trod descends across ploughing

terraces to a small parking area beside the bend of a lane (the alternative start point) **C**.

The way back is to the right, but first clamber up onto Scratchbury Hill, where there is another hilltop fort. Take the lane opposite, but then leave at the corner of a short fence for a path signed off right beside it up onto the hill. The way begins to climb fairly steeply, passing through a kissing-gate part-way up and eventually reaching the embankment defences. Having gained the height, wander round the perimeter to enjoy the views before heading back down to the bend of the road **C**.

Instead of following the lane down to

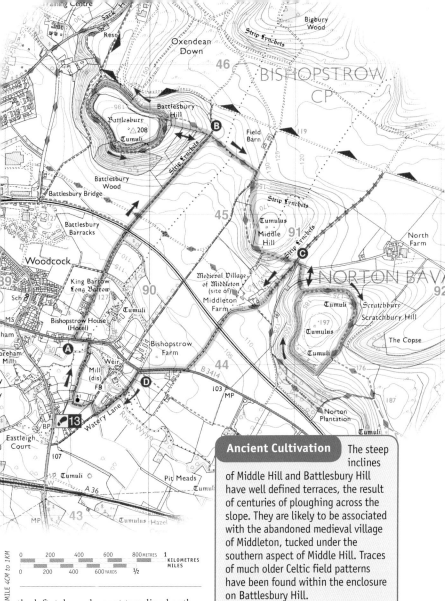

SCALE 1:25 000 or 2½ INCHES to 1 MILE 4CM to 1KM

| 0 | 200 | 400 | 600 | 800 METRES | 1 |
| 0 | 200 | 400 | 600 YARDS | ½ | KILOMETRES / MILES |

Ancient Cultivation

The steep inclines of Middle Hill and Battlesbury Hill have well defined terraces, the result of centuries of ploughing across the slope. They are likely to be associated with the abandoned medieval village of Middleton, tucked under the southern aspect of Middle Hill. Traces of much older Celtic field patterns have been found within the enclosure on Battlesbury Hill.

the left, take a pleasant tree-lined path that leaves from the corner of the parking area. The trail falls away along the base of a fold, passing below the abandoned medieval village of Middleton, which lay above the trees up to your right. The path comes out beside a tile-topped wall at Middleton Farm. Bear right to join a lane from the farm, carry on downhill, passing beneath the railway and ultimately meeting the main road.

Go right as far as a bend **D**, carefully crossing left to Watery Lane. Follow it down to the entrance of 'Waterways' and then branch off left on a grass path. In 200 yards, keep your eyes peeled for a small stream. There, turn off right beside it on a narrow path, the church soon coming into view. The path angles through to the corner of the village cricket pitch. Follow a wall round its right edge back to the churchyard gate.

walk 14

Start
Stourton

Distance
6¼ miles (10.1km)

Height gain
885 feet (270m)

Approximate time
3¼ hours

Route terrain
Woodland tracks and meadow paths, some lane

P Parking
National Trust car park, Stourton (Pay & Display). Alternative NT car park at Alfred's Tower

OS maps
Landranger 183 (Yeovil & Frome), Explorer 142 (Shepton Mallet & Mendip Hills East)

GPS waypoints
- ST 779 340
- Ⓐ ST 771 346
- Ⓑ ST 766 340
- Ⓒ ST 755 342
- Ⓓ ST 748 342
- Ⓔ ST 743 350
- Ⓕ ST 745 351
- Ⓖ ST 751 353
- Ⓗ ST 772 338

Stourton and King Alfred's Tower

Connecting Stourton with the striking monument of King Alfred's Tower on Kingsettle Hill, this walk wanders through the woods of the Stourhead estate. But there are plenty of open spaces and pastures too from which there are grand views across the countryside, while the National Trust's gardens, lake and Stourhead House itself are all worth a visit.

Return to the road from the car park and head left. After 100 yards, turn off right through a grand, castellated gateway into Stourhead Park. The drive winds away, passing the walled gardens and stables and then the grand Palladian mansion itself. At a junction beyond, go left with the Stour Valley Way across the open park, an obelisk coming into view on the left.

When the track later swings right, through a gate to a lodge, look for a path off left over a stile Ⓐ. Head down steps, passing steeply through trees, swing right towards the bottom, and down steps to come out at the edge of the wood. Go right to find a stile on the left, over which, head downhill across open ground to pass along a small dam between pools in the base of the valley. In a few paces, branching right on a narrow path, climb steeply into the trees. Eventually cresting the hill by a bench, cross a wide glade, keeping slightly left to pick up the path again into the trees. Cross another two wide rides before the way descends, ultimately losing height more steeply to a

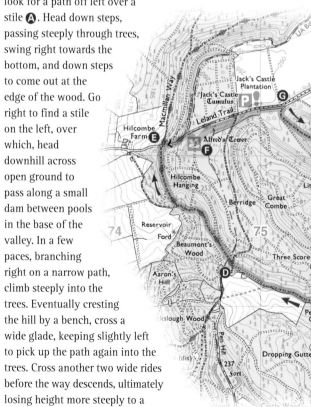

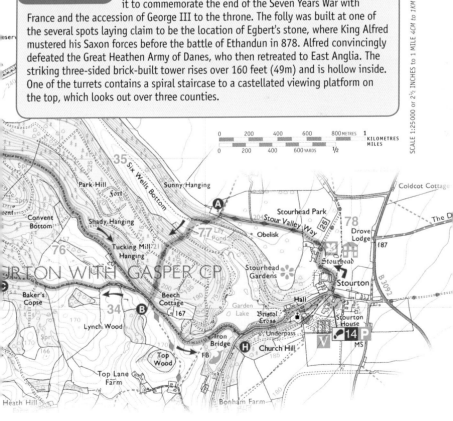
The entrance to the park

crossing track at the far side of the forest **B**.

Follow it to the right, soon reaching a fork. Take the left branch, heading gently downhill and crossing a stream. Climbing beyond, the track shortly leads into an open field. Keep ahead, the path rising alongside the left

---

Alfred's Tower

The tower was erected in 1772 by Henry Hoare II, who raised it to commemorate the end of the Seven Years War with France and the accession of George III to the throne. The folly was built at one of the several spots laying claim to be the location of Egbert's stone, where King Alfred mustered his Saxon forces before the battle of Ethandun in 878. Alfred convincingly defeated the Great Heathen Army of Danes, who then retreated to East Anglia. The striking three-sided brick-built tower rises over 160 feet (49m) and is hollow inside. One of the turrets contains a spiral staircase to a castellated viewing platform on the top, which looks out over three counties.

SCALE 1:25000 or 2½ INCHES to 1 MILE 4CM to 1KM

boundary and, in time, passing over a stile into more trees. Follow the track ahead, which soon meets the bend of a gravel forest road **C**.

Go left and wind round the edge of mixed woodland. After ½ mile (800m), keep ahead at a fork, walking on to a second junction a short distance farther on **D**. Take the track ahead, and at the next junction keep left, the way undulating as it parallels the woodland fringe. At the subsequent intersection, continue ahead and then, just beyond, go right at a fork, the track now steadily gaining height through Hilcombe Hanging. Ignore any side paths and carry on, the gradient eventually easing before falling to meet a narrow lane **E**.

Follow it up to the right, climbing steeply once more. Before long, however, the lane levels at the top of the hill and you can leave through a break in the trees on the right to an open meadow, the Terrace Ride. Ahead

in the clearing rises the imposing structure of King Alfred's Tower **F**.

After ascending the spiral staircase to savour the fantastic view from the top, continue east along the Terrace Ride for about 650 yards. Pass two prominent tracks off to the right, but at a third **G**, just beyond a small clearing set back on the right, take it into the trees. Keep left past an almost immediate fork and follow the onward trail, steadily descending along the base of a wooded valley. Ignoring side paths, the way later becomes more open as it runs at the edge of the trees and ultimately, after some 1¼ miles (2km), returns you to a junction, passed earlier in the walk. Keep ahead, briefly retracing your outward steps and passing the spot where you initially joined the track **B**. Keep forward over a stile.

Before long, the track winds round beside a narrow arm of Garden Lake. The way then curves right over a dam

The waterwheel

holding the water back above Turner's Paddock Lake, passing a waterwheel and pump house, to emerge onto a lane **H**. Go left, passing beneath an ornamental bridge and walk on uphill back to the car park. Passed along the way is the Bristol Cross to the left, while St Peter's Church and **The Spread Eagle** are just beyond on the right. You can avoid the rest of the lane by turning off into a courtyard immediately beyond the inn. Swing left to leave through a covered passage and across the inn's car park from which a path leads back to the main car park. ●

Pewsey Downs

The first part of the walk descends from Walkers Hill, high up on the Pewsey Downs overlooking the Vale of Pewsey, and passes through the adjoining hamlets of Alton Priors and Alton Barnes, both with ancient churches, to the Kennet and Avon Canal at Honeystreet. After a walk along the canal, the route continues into Stanton St Bernard and then ascends Milk Hill. On the final exhilarating downland stretch there are more grand views over the vale. The climb back on to the downs is gradual but with one fairly steep section.

From the car park cross the road and go through the gate opposite. Immediately turn left over a stile and walk across the grass, initially by a wire fence bordering the road on the left, later veering slightly right to a stile. Climb it and head diagonally left uphill and over a stile. Keep ahead across the down, passing to the right of Adam's Grave, a prehistoric long barrow which the Saxons called Woden's Barrow, on top of the hill. At the top head south and below you is the outline of the path running down the hillside towards the villages of Alton Priors and Alton Barnes. Make for a gate, here leaving Pewsey Down Nature Reserve, continue down a path to the road, turn left uphill and after 200 yards, turn sharp right along the White Horse Trail **A**, here a narrow sunken path between trees, running gently downhill between two fields. If overgrown follow parallel field edge. Later continue along a tarmac track to emerge on to a road in the hamlet of Alton Priors. Turn left, immediately turn right **B** along a lane, and where it ends pass through a wooden turnstile – the first of several on the next stage of the walk.

Keep ahead, passing to the right of Alton Priors church. This mainly dates from the 14th century but the interior is dominated by the fine Norman chancel arch. Continue along a paved path, go through a turnstile, cross two footbridges in quick succession and go through another turnstile. Follow the path over a path junction, head diagonally across a field and go through the last of the turnstiles on to a lane in Alton Barnes. To the left is the tiny church which is of Saxon origin, restored by the Victorians.

The route continues to the right along the lane to a T-junction **C**. Here turn left along the road into the canal

walk 15

Start
Walkers Hill

Distance
6¾ miles (10.9km)

Height gain
740 feet (225m)

Approximate time
3½ hours

Route terrain
Undulating downland; canal towpath. Approach to Alton Barnes can be overgrown. One steep climb to the Wansdyke

P Parking
Car park at the top of the hill on the road between Alton Barnes and Lockeridge

OS maps
Landranger 173 (Swindon & Devizes), Explorer 157 (Marlborough & Savernake Forest)

GPS waypoints
SU 115 638
A SU 112 629
B SU 110 623
C SU 105 620
D SU 104 615
E SU 089 620
F SU 095 626
G SU 096 635
H SU 101 644
J SU 102 646

settlement of Honeystreet, which was built in 1811 just after the opening of the Kennet and Avon canal. Remains of the wharf can still be seen. Cross the canal bridge, immediately turn right **D** to descend to the towpath and walk along it, passing the **Barge Inn**. Over to the right the White Horse of Alton Barnes, which dates from 1812, can be seen on the side of the downs. Pass under the second bridge, immediately turn left up to a track and turn left again **E** to cross the bridge. Follow the track to the left and, in front of Riding School buildings, turn right and then left to reach a lane at a bend. Turn right through the village of Stanton St Bernard, passing to the left of the church – mainly 19th-century except for the medieval tower – and follow the lane round right- and left-hand bends.

After a sharp right bend look out for Coate Road on the left, and turn left by Corner Cottage along it. Follow the lane as it bears left, then right, to meet a T-junction. Turn right along the road. At a public footpath sign and White Horse waymark, turn left **F** and keep straight ahead across huge fields, aiming for the left end of Milk Hill. Cross a track and continue to where the path bends left. Two gates are seen here. Immediately beyond them turn left **G** along the bottom edge of the down, by a wire fence on the left which gradually curves to the right. Just before reaching the field corner, and a group of hawthorns, bear right and head steadily uphill, by a wire fence on the left. Go through a gap and continue more steeply uphill. Head towards a fence on the skyline and as you approach it, follow the path round to the left. Go through a gate and continue with the fence on the right. Pass through another gate (signs here for the Mid Wilts Way and Whitehorse Trail) **H**. Keep along the fence to the next gate **J**. Turn right and follow a

The White Horse of Alton Barnes from the canal

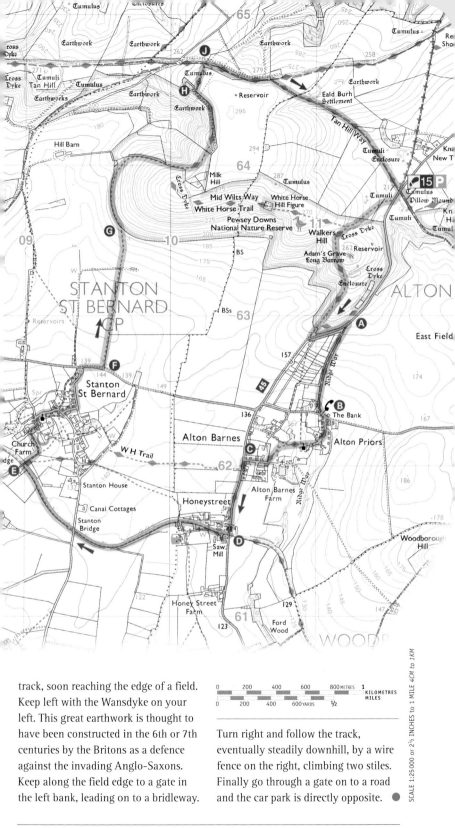

track, soon reaching the edge of a field. Keep left with the Wansdyke on your left. This great earthwork is thought to have been constructed in the 6th or 7th centuries by the Britons as a defence against the invading Anglo-Saxons. Keep along the field edge to a gate in the left bank, leading on to a bridleway.

Turn right and follow the track, eventually steadily downhill, by a wire fence on the right, climbing two stiles. Finally go through a gate on to a road and the car park is directly opposite. ●

| 0 | 200 | 400 | 600 | 800 METRES | 1 |
| 0 | 200 | 400 | 600 YARDS | ½ | |

SCALE 1:25000 or 2½ INCHES to 1 MILE 4CM to 1KM

walk 16

Start

Bradford-on-Avon

Distance

7 miles (11.3km)

Height gain

605 feet (185m)

Approximate time

3½ hours

Route terrain

Canal towpath and farmland paths. One steep climb before the walk joins the road near Westwood. Steeply descending field and woodland paths to Avoncliff

P Parking

Bradford-on-Avon

OS maps

Landrangers 172 (Bristol & Bath) and 173 (Swindon & Devizes), Explorer 156 (Chippenham & Bradford-on-Avon)

GPS waypoints

- ST 826 608
- Ⓐ ST 815 603
- Ⓑ ST 813 598
- Ⓒ ST 812 589
- Ⓓ ST 811 577
- Ⓔ ST 803 577
- Ⓕ ST 805 580
- Ⓖ ST 800 592
- Ⓗ ST 804 599

Bradford-on-Avon, Westwood and Avoncliff

This is a walk of great interest, scenic beauty and variety. It includes attractive waterside stretches along the banks of the rivers Avon and Frome and the Kennet and Avon Canal, farmland, woodland and superb views over both the Frome and Avon valleys. Historic interest is provided by the Saxon church, bridge chapel and tithe barn at Bradford-on-Avon, church and manor at Westwood, ruins of Farleigh Hungerford Castle (which involves a short detour), and the aqueduct at Avoncliff. Some muddy stretches can be expected. Allow plenty of time in order to enjoy this absorbing walk to the full.

Wool is a common link between Bradford-on-Avon and its larger Yorkshire namesake but there the similarity ends. While the northern Bradford expanded into a major industrial city during the Victorian era, Bradford-on-Avon declined, though the imposing 19th-century Abbey Mill would not look out of place in a Pennine valley. The result of this decline is a highly attractive town, sloping steeply down the sides of the valley to the river, with many fine stone buildings belonging to the 16th, 17th and 18th centuries, the heyday of the local Cotswold woollen trade.

The oldest building is the tiny Saxon church, a striking contrast to the imposing medieval church nearby. Built in the 10th century or even earlier, it is one of the best preserved Anglo-Saxon churches in England and was only rediscovered in the 19th century, having been used as a cottage and schoolroom. The medieval Town Bridge over the Avon has a rare chapel on it, later used as a lock up; the walk starts on the south side of this bridge.

Walk away from the bridge, passing the War Memorial gardens on the right, and turn right, at a sign for short stay car parking and swimming pool, into a car park. *For a short detour to visit the churches, bear right and cross a footbridge.* Turn left in front of St Margaret's Hall and take the paved riverside path, passing to the right of **Timbrell's Yard**, to follow a pleasant wooded stretch of the Avon.

Pass under a railway bridge and at a T-junction turn right along a tarmac track through Barton Farm Country Park, a thin strip of land between river and canal that extends from Bradford to Avoncliff. Over to the left is the magnificent tithe barn, 168 feet (51m) long, built in the 14th century to store produce for the nuns of Shaftesbury Abbey. Keep beside the river and after ½ mile (800m), the track bears left (signposted Avoncliff via towpath) uphill to cross a footbridge over the Kennet and Avon Canal **Ⓐ**. Turn right beside the canal – this path may be muddy – cross a footbridge to a kissing-gate, continue along the right edge of a field and make for a kissing-gate in the field corner. Bear slightly left away from the canal and head uphill across the next field towards trees. Do not go through a metal kissing-gate into the trees but turn sharp left and continue along the top edge of the field. From here there is a good view over the town. Continue to a stile, keep going to the next, cross a paddock to a kissing-gate and then continue ahead for a few paces to a stone stile. Follow an enclosed path to the left of a bungalow on to a lane **Ⓑ**.

Cross over, climb a double stile and go diagonally across the field. About 50 yards before the field corner you

The River Avon at Bradford-on-Avon

reach two stiles on the right; climb the first (right-hand one) and continue

along the left edge of fields, by a hedge on the left, and eventually emerging on to a lane at Westwood. Continue along the lane to a T-junction, cross over, go up steps, through a kissing-gate and

SCALE 1:25000 or 2½ INCHES to 1 MILE 4CM to 1KM

| 0 | 200 | 400 | 600 | 800 METRES | 1 KILOMETRES |
| 0 | 200 | 400 | 600 YARDS | ½ | MILES |

BRADFORD-ON-AVON

Hill View Farm

Turleigh

Belcombe Court

Turleigh Farm

River Avon

Tithe Barn

A

Sewage Farm

Kennet and Avon Canal

Avoncliff Station

Barton Farm Country Park

Air Shaft

H

Weir

Avoncliff

Leigh Green Farm

B

Lye Green

Air Shaft

Upper Westwood

WESTWOOD CP

Superstore

Westwood

Sch

Lower Westwood

Elms Cross Vineyard

Hudds Farm

G

Macmillan Way

PO

Cemy

Manor House

C

Manor Farm

Iford Manor Bridge

Iford Mill

Haygrove Plantation

Midway Manor

Oxstall Farm

Weir

Sewage Works

Rowley Copse

Medieval Village of Rowley (site of)

Trowle Wo

Rowley Manor

F

Quarry (dis)

Farleigh Castle (rems of)

Quarry (dis)

WINGFIELD

Frome Road

Trowle Farm

E

Weir

Stowford Farm

D

A 366

Farleigh Hungerford

Wingfield House

Castle Farm

Snarlton Farm

War Meml

Wingfield

Golf Driving Range

Weir

Pomeroy Lane

Belle Coeur Farm

Matthews Farm

walk along an enclosed path. Turn left and follow the path beside a wall into the churchyard, continue through it and go through a metal gate on to a lane **C**.

The dominant feature of Westwood's mainly 15th-century church is the tall west tower. To the left is Westwood Manor, also 15th-century but with Tudor and Jacobean additions. It is now owned by the National Trust. Further along the lane to the left is the **New Inn**.

Climb a metal stile opposite, head straight across a field, following the direction of a public footpath sign to Stowford, pass to the left of a circular, tree-fringed pond and go through a gap to continue across the next field. Climb a stile, continue across the next field, go through a metal gate and down the field curving to the right to a gap into the next pasture. Turn immediately left to a second gap, then swing right on to a track, follow it down to a farm and on to a road **D**. Turn right, in 50 yards turn left along the drive to Stowford Manor Farm and immediately turn right to head across grass to a stile. The next part of the route is along a permissive path. Climb the stile and continue across a series of narrow fields, between the road on the right and the River Frome on the left, eventually climbing a stile on to a road to the right of a bridge **E**.

The route continues to the right but *turn left uphill if you wish to make a brief detour to visit Farleigh Hungerford Castle*. This was built in the late 14th-century by Sir Thomas Hungerford and was later extended, taking over the entire village in the process. The Hungerfords built a new village and church, with the old church becoming the castle chapel.

On emerging on to the road turn right, not along the main road which curves to the right but along a narrow, uphill lane. Opposite a small lay-by, turn left **F** on to a track through trees. Continue along this pleasant, enclosed track from which there are fine views to the left over the Frome Valley. Later the track becomes tree-lined. Continue ahead and eventually reach a stone wall on the left, followed by a lane. Turn sharp right here, climb steeply round to the left and continue on the higher ground. Pass Iford Fields on the right and at the T-junction, turn left along the road by the entrance to **Iford Manor Gardens**, which are open to the public at various times.

After $^1/_4$ mile (400m) turn right **G**, at a public bridleway sign to Upper Westwood, along a hedge-lined path to a road. Turn right and after a few yards turn left along a track between houses to a gate. Ahead is a glorious view over the Avon Valley. Go through the gate, head downhill along the right edge of a field and in the field corner turn right through a kissing-gate into trees. A few yards ahead turn sharp left, do not go through the kissing-gate in front but follow the path to the right and head down to climb a stile into a field. Continue downhill, making for a kissing-gate in the bottom right-hand corner, and then walk along a track by a wall on the right. Follow the track into Avoncliff and the river is below on the left.

Pass under the Avoncliff Aqueduct, which was built by John Rennie in 1810 to take the canal across the Avon Valley, then head up to the **Cross Guns** and turn sharp right up to the aqueduct **H**. Turn left, here re-entering Barton Farm Country Park, and follow the quiet, tree-lined towpath back to Bradford-on-Avon.

At the first footbridge **A** you rejoin the outward route – bear left down the tarmac track to the river and retrace your steps to the start. ●

walk 17

Start

Lacock

Distance

7 miles (11.3km)

Height gain

690 feet (210m)

Approximate time

3½ hours

Route terrain

Deceptively strenuous walk through undulating countryside

P Parking

National Trust car park at Lacock

OS maps

Landranger 173 (Swindon & Devizes), Explorer 156 (Chippenham & Bradford-on-Avon)

GPS waypoints

ST 918 682
Ⓐ ST 919 691
Ⓑ ST 944 702
Ⓒ ST 933 692
Ⓓ ST 931 683
Ⓔ ST 924 680

Lacock and Bowden Park

This is a walk across fields and through woodland in the gentle countryside of the Avon Valley to the north and east of the National Trust village of Lacock. There are some splendid views, especially on the descent through Bowden Park, and a pleasant finale across riverside meadows. Expect some overgrown and muddy paths in places and, as this is a fairly tortuous route, follow the directions carefully.

Cross the road from the car park and take the path through the trees, signposted 'Village, Abbey Museum and Shops'. At a road, turn left into Lacock. Renowned as one of England's most beautiful villages, Lacock is a harmonious mixture of stone and half-timbered buildings spanning the centuries from the 13th to the 19th. Like many of the nearby Cotswold villages, its wealth and prosperity were based on the medieval wool trade. One of its finest buildings is the mainly 14th- and 15th-century church, unusual in that although cruciform, it has a west tower and spire.

Lacock Abbey was originally an Augustinian monastery, founded in 1232, and when it was converted into a Tudor mansion after its closure in 1539, some of the medieval monastic buildings, including the cloisters and chapter house, were incorporated into the new structure. Further alterations were made in the 18th and 19th centuries. In the middle years of the 19th century it was the home of William Henry Fox Talbot, pioneer of modern photography, and there is a museum commemorating his work near the abbey entrance. Both abbey and village were given to the National Trust in 1944.

Turn right opposite the **Red Lion**, at a T-junction turn right again and in front of the church turn left along a lane, at a No Through Road sign. Cross a footbridge over a brook, by a ford, then at a fork take the right-hand tarmac path to rejoin the lane. Walk uphill to where the lane ends in front of a fence.

Take the path to the right, passing through a kissing-gate, and follow a tarmac path across a field to another kissing-gate on the far side. Go through, continue along an enclosed path to a road, keep ahead for a few yards and turn right to cross the bridge over the River Avon **Ⓐ**. Turn left over a stile, at a public footpath sign, and walk diagonally across a field, making for a metal stile. Climb it, cross a tarmac drive, climb a metal stile opposite and keep along a narrow, enclosed path. The path curves right, then bends left and you climb two more metal stiles in quick succession before emerging into a field.

Turn left along the field edge, follow it to the right, and look out for a double stile in the hedge on the left. Cross both

and turn right to keep along the top edge of the next field, now with the hedge on the right. Continue to a stile; over it, walk an enclosed path to another stile. Turn left over this to join a tarmac path, alongside the partly restored Wilts. and Berks. Canal. To the left is the winding River Avon.

Continue to a bridge, opened by the Duchess of Cornwall in 2009. Cross over and turn left to pass over a stile into a field. Keep ahead along the left-hand edge of the field to a stile and gateway. Go over this and cross the next field to a stile leading to an overgrown path through trees. On the far side of the

SCALE 1:25000 or 2½ INCHES to 1 MILE 4CM to 1KM

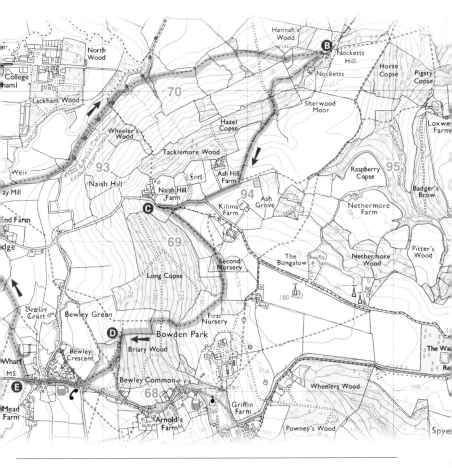

trees, cross a stile and go straight ahead across the field. Keep ahead and soon you are alongside trees and boundary hedge on the left. Head towards a house on the skyline, make for a gateway and in the next field turn left to skirt its perimeter, heading for a metal gate on the right of woodland. Go through and continue along the left edge of the next field, cross a track, then bear slightly right away from the field edge and head diagonally uphill to a stile in the far corner.

Climb it and bear right in the field, crossing a stile by a metal gate en route. A few yards in front of a metal gate in the top left corner of the field (with a house beyond) turn sharp right **B** and head back along the top edge of the field just crossed. Passing over a ditch reach a metal hand-gate. Through this, walk across the next field, bearing left to join a tarmac track running into woodland. Turn left over a cattle-grid, head gently uphill through the wood, emerging from the trees at a cattle-grid.

Continue along the track, at first along the right edge of a field and then heading gently uphill across fields and curving right over a cattle-grid. Go through, continue along the track – now enclosed – to a narrow lane and turn right along it. Follow it as it descends and as it bears right, turn left over a stile **C**. From here there is a grand view over the Avon Valley.

After climbing the stile turn sharp left to keep along the left edge of a field, then bear slightly away from it to go through a metal gate and continue by a wire fence along the left edge of the next field. Climb a stile in the corner to enter woodland, continue through it to a stile. Climb it, keep by woodland and a hedge along the right edge of a field, and just before reaching the field corner, turn right over a waymarked stile.

Head diagonally downhill across Bowden Park – there is a superb view ahead over the Avon Valley with the 18th-century house to the left. Bear gradually right towards the bottom corner of the woodland on the right, and aim for the gap between two belts of woodland. In the bottom right-hand corner of the field, turn right along a track to a stile, climb it, continue downhill across a field and climb another stile beside a gate. Turn left towards woodland, then swing right in front of the trees to keep parallel to them. Make for the woodland corner by a house **D**. Climb a stile and continue along an enclosed track, which continues across open ground. Where it bears left towards a gatehouse, bear right and head diagonally across the open expanse of Bewley Common to a road.

Turn right along it, heading gently downhill all the while, and about 200 yards before reaching the bridge over the river, turn right over a stile **E**, at a public footpath sign, and head across the riverside meadows. To the left Lacock Abbey is glimpsed across the Avon. Bear right towards the hedge on the right edge of the meadow and look out for a footbridge over a ditch and a stile. Climb the stile, keep by a hedge along the left edge of a field, go through a metal gate and bear slightly right across the next field, making for a hedge gap, metal gate and public footpath sign. Climb a stile to the left of the gate and keep ahead by the banks of the placid Avon.

Go through a gate, keep ahead across the meadow – cutting a corner where the river does a loop to the left – and continue to a stile to the right of the bridge. Climb it on to a road, turn left over the bridge **A** and retrace your steps left, bearing left again for the path back to Lacock. ●

Ludgershall Castle

Although relatively little known beyond its locality nowadays, Ludgershall was once the playground of royalty, its medieval castle given new life as a hunting lodge and a favourite resort of King James. Today's forest is managed as a cash crop, but there is still plenty of wildlife about in the remoter valleys and glades.

Out of the car park, go right along St James Street. Immediately beyond the church, take a path off left that leads through to another street. Walk right and bear left to the main road, crossing to a track opposite. Beyond barns, carry on at the field edge, eventually meeting a crossing path **A**.

Turn left, but then shortly branch off right at the edge of a field and continue beside Heron's Copse. At the point where the edge of the wood later curves away, pass through a gate on the right. Keep going beside the boundary of the wood to reach its northern tip, there swinging left at the field edge to the top corner. Pass through a gap into the adjacent field and then exit through a gate on the left onto a track **B**.

Follow it to the right, shortly passing a trig pillar, which stands in the field over to the left. Ignore a crossing track by barns and carry on, eventually meeting a bridleway fringed by trees **C**. Go right for ¼ mile (400m) but, just past a field gate on the left, look for a waymarked bridlepath leaving left and climbing gently at the edge of the wood. After 600 yards, watch for a lowered section of fence on the left, a horse jump **D**. At

walk 18

Start
Ludgershall

Distance
7¼ miles (11.7km)

Height gain
640 feet (195m)

Approximate time
3½ hours

Route terrain
Woodland paths and tracks

Parking
Car park in St James Street

OS maps
Landranger 184 (Salisbury & The Plain), Explorer 131 (Romsey, Andover & Test Valley)

GPS waypoints
SU 264 508
A SU 263 516
B SU 260 527
C SU 261 535
D SU 267 539
E SU 285 539
F SU 284 530
G SU 282 526
H SU 272 514

Ludgershall Castle

that point, take a path on the right heading into the forest. Ignore a later crossing path and carry on as far again to reach a broad track, Water Lane.

Cross to the ongoing path opposite, which rises easily through the trees and in due course meets another junction at the eastern edge of the forest. Walk on ahead, leaving the forest through a gate into a field. Strike across to the corner of a wood opposite and continue beside it down to Shaw Bottom. Exit the corner of the field through a gate on the left onto the bend of a track. Follow it right, climbing straight up the opposite side of the valley.

Just beyond the crest, as the track bends left, turn off through a waymarked gate on the right **E**. Walk away half-right and then curve left on a grass trod. Approaching a grass bank, an ancient earthwork, bear off left beside it and carry on towards a clump of trees. There wind left and right round it to discover a gate in the corner and continue along an enclosed path, the bank and ditch now hidden in the bushes to the right.

Through a gateway, ignore a crossing path, almost immediately passing beneath a pylon and into the forest. Stick with the obvious path, gently falling through the trees and eventually winding down to meet a crossing path **F**. Follow it left.

Before long, the track broadens and leads to a junction. Keep ahead and stay with the main track as it swings right and follow it down for ¼ mile (400m) into a dip. As the trail then begins to climb, watch for a crossing path **G**.

Take it, leaving between posts to the left. It winds through towards the fringe of the wood. As the path then swings left, turn off sharp right on another path running west just within the trees. Before long it leads to a wayposted junction. Branch left there, breaking out onto the edge of a field. Follow a broad swathe away to the right, over a slight rise and then gently downhill. Passing through a narrow belt of trees, continue at the perimeter of a second field. In time, reaching a barrier by the corner of the wood, go right through a gap and walk between a hedge and the edge of the trees to a small gate into another field. Head away beside the left hedge, turning left round its corner to another gate, from which a contained path leads out onto a junction by Crawlboys Farm **H**.

Turn sharp right along a stone bridleway track, but where that ultimately turns right up to Woods Farm, abandon it through a signed gap on the left. Walk away at the edge of a field over a rise and down to pass a house. Leave just beyond it through a gate on the right onto the end of a drive. Follow that away, bending round past the castle and out to join the main road. Walk forward, shortly reaching the old market preaching cross in front of the **Queens Head**. Although its faces are much eroded, it is just possible to make out their depictions, which have been interpreted as; (clockwise from the north), the Ascension, the descent from the cross, the Road to Emmaus, and the harrowing of hell. Cross the road and turn into Church Lane, going left at the end back to the car park. ●

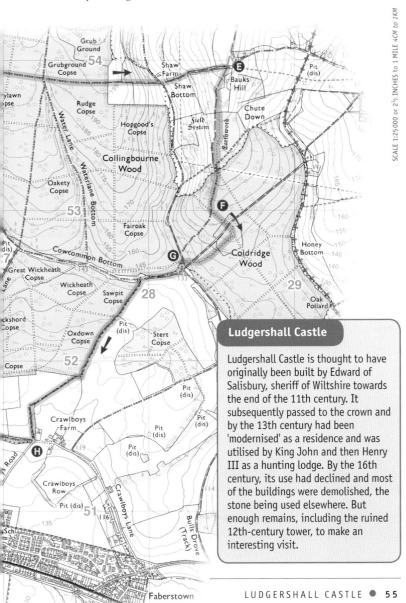

Ludgershall Castle

Ludgershall Castle is thought to have originally been built by Edward of Salisbury, sheriff of Wiltshire towards the end of the 11th century. It subsequently passed to the crown and by the 13th century had been 'modernised' as a residence and was utilised by King John and then Henry III as a hunting lodge. By the 16th century, its use had declined and most of the buildings were demolished, the stone being used elsewhere. But enough remains, including the ruined 12th-century tower, to make an interesting visit.

SCALE 1:25 000 or 2½ INCHES to 1 MILE 4CM to 1KM

Avebury, West Kennett and Silbury Hill

Start
Avebury

Distance
7½ miles (12.1km)

Height gain
460 feet (140m)

Approximate time
3½ hours

Route terrain
Downland tracks; gently undulating meadow and field paths

Parking
National Trust car park at Avebury

OS maps
Landranger 173 (Swindon & Devizes), Explorer 157 (Marlborough & Savernake Forest)

GPS waypoints
SU 099 696
Ⓐ SU 100 699
Ⓑ SU 125 708
Ⓒ SU 118 680
Ⓓ SU 119 674
Ⓔ SU 114 678
Ⓕ SU 104 681

This fascinating walk links the most outstanding collection of prehistoric remains in the country. From the stone circle at Avebury, the route heads up on to the downs and follows a section of the Ridgeway into the village of East Kennett. It then continues to the impressive West Kennett Long Barrow, and the final stretch, mainly by the infant River Kennet, takes you past the intriguing Silbury Hill, the largest artificial mound in Europe. Allow plenty of time in order to appreciate these unique monuments to the full.

A 17th-century antiquarian wrote of the great stone circle at Avebury that 'it did as much excel Stonehenge, as a cathedral does a parish church'. Constructed sometime between 2700 and 1700BC and the focal point of the most important group of prehistoric monuments in the country, it is undeniably impressive, even in an incomplete state. It is also more complex than it seems, with two smaller circles within the main outer ring of stones, and protected by a ditch and embankment. The size of the circle and the proximity of the other monuments suggest that it must have been a major political and/or religious centre of Neolithic Britain.

Partially enclosed by the stone circle, the village of Avebury is a most attractive place in its own right, with an Elizabethan manor house and fine medieval church.

Begin along a tarmac path, signposted to the Stone Circle, which winds from the far corner of the car park past a cricket field to emerge in the village Ⓐ. After exploring the surrounding henge and stone circles, walk to the main road and past the **Red Lion** to leave on the next bend, heading east along Green Street from the village. Beyond the outer bank of the henge and later, a farm, the lane degrades to a rough track, which rises steadily towards the ridge.

After 1½ miles (2.5km), at a crossing, turn right along the Ridgeway Ⓑ. Follow a gently descending track across the downs, from which there are wide-ranging views. Eventually, passing a group of tumuli in a field on the left, the track leads to the busy A4 road Ⓒ.

| 0 | 200 | 400 | 600 | 800 METRES | 1 |
| 0 | 200 | 400 | 600 YARDS | ½ | |

KILOMETRES
MILES

Cross to the ongoing track opposite where, just along on the right, a gate opens to the Sanctuary. The monument was originally set out as a double circle of wood and later rebuilt in stone, but the posts have long since decayed and the stones were destroyed by farmers in the 18th century. Concrete markers have been placed to show their original positions and allow an appreciation of the scale of the monument. It was linked to the henge at Avebury by a processional avenue of stones, some of which survive beside the lane between West Kennett and Avebury.

Carry on along the enclosed track, which runs downhill between trees, hedgerows and fields. Reaching the bottom, wind left to a bridge over the infant River Kennet and continue along a tarmac drive to a lane at the edge of East Kennett. Walk ahead for a few yards before turning off right at a wall corner **D** along an enclosed path that cuts through to another lane. Go right again and wander through the village. Approaching a small substation and bridge over the River Kennet, turn off along a track on the left.

After 200 yards, and just past a track off left, look for a narrow path; it is waymarked into the trees on the right **E**. Entering a field, walk beside the left boundary, remaining by the hedge as it later bends to the left. Over another stile at the far end, cross a minor lane and continue with the track opposite. Where that ends, keep along the bottom edge of a large field to reach a junction by a solitary oak **F**.

Turn left and head steadily up to the West Kennett Long Barrow, which can be seen near the top of the hill. This stone-chambered tomb, dating from around 3700BC and nearly 350 feet (106m) long is the largest burial chamber in England. The three huge stones guarding the entrance were possibly placed there when the tomb was sealed up.

Retracing your steps down the hill, the view is dominated by the imposing bulk of Silbury Hill. At the bottom, go left and then right through a metal kissing-gate to a bridge over the river.

Keep ahead through another gate out to the A4 road. Cross to a signposted gate diagonally opposite and follow a field-edge path left, running parallel to the road. Over a bridge, continue in the next field, but return to the road at the far end. Follow the pavement on past the massive mound of Silbury Hill, and then look for a narrow path leaving through the trees; it emerges by a viewing area and information board.

Silbury Hill is the largest prehistoric man-made mound in Europe, 130 feet (39m) high and covering an area of over 5 acres (2 ha). So well built was it that there has hardly been any erosion over a period of nearly 5,000 years. Investigations and excavations have failed to find out the exact purpose of this incredible feat of construction and it remains one of the great mysteries of prehistory.

Turn towards a car park, but as you approach, swing off right on a grass swathe through the trees to find a contained path running away between the fields. Over a bridge at the end, go left on a crossing path that leads back to Avebury, emerging onto the A4361 road almost opposite the car park.

The stones of West Kennett Long Barrow

Tollard Royal and Win Green

walk 20

Start
Tollard Royal

Distance
6¾ miles (10.9km)

Height gain
970 feet (295m)

Approximate time
3½ hours

Route terrain
Undulating downland tracks and paths

P Parking
By village pond at Tollard Royal. Alternatively, park at the NT's Win Green car park and begin the walk from **C**

OS maps
Landranger 184 (Salisbury & The Plain), Explorer 118 (Shaftesbury & Cranborne Chase)

GPS waypoints
📷 ST 944 178
A ST 936 186
B ST 930 203
C ST 925 206
D ST 937 207
E ST 948 206
F ST 951 176

From the village of Tollard Royal near the Dorset border, several wooded valleys lead up on to a ridge. This route takes one of these, climbing steadily and quite steeply at times, to reach Win Green hill – at 911 feet (277m) the highest point on Cranborne Chase and a magnificent vantage point. This is followed by a splendid ridge walk, with more outstanding views, and a descent via a parallel valley to return to the start.

Close to the medieval church in Tollard Royal is King John's House – originally a 13th-century hunting lodge, it was remodelled in the 16th century and restored during the Victorian era. Its name indicates that Cranborne Chase, an area of wooded valleys and rolling chalk uplands on the borders of Wiltshire and Dorset, was originally a royal forest – a favourite hunting ground of King John and other medieval monarchs. It became a private chase in the early 17th century when James I bestowed it upon Robert Cecil, Earl of Salisbury.

📷 Start by taking the tarmac track to the left of the pond and, after a few paces keep left at a fork by some outbuildings. The track heads steadily uphill, to a kissing-gate. Go through it and continue by a wire fence on the left and after going through a metal gate, the track descends. After a few paces, turn right through a gate and cross a narrow neck of grass to a further gate. Turn right **A** along a track that continues through Ashcombe Bottom. At a fork, take the left-hand track and follow it as it passes to the right of a cottage.

On the next part of the walk there are two forks in fairly quick succession; in both cases you take the left-hand track, following a series of green metal footpath posts. The track bends right and ascends steeply. At a footpath sign bend left and follow it uphill – here the climb is steep. Pass a private estate sign for oncoming walkers, go through a kissing-gate ahead and head out on to open grassland **B**. Continue uphill, passing a waymarked post, and later keep left alongside a wire fence on the left. Reach a stile, turn right over it, and head across to the triangulation pillar and toposcope on the top of Win Green hill, 911 feet (277m) **C**. From here, the highest point on Cranborne Chase, the magnificent all-round views extend across the wooded slopes of the chase to the Mendips,

Marlborough Downs, New Forest, Dorset coast and even the Isle of Wight.

Walk past the triangulation pillar, passing to the left of a tree-encircled tumulus, and bear slightly right round the curve of the tumulus to continue along a broad grassy downhill track with a field gate at the bottom. Pass beside this and turn right to join a main track – there now follows an exhilarating ridge top walk, with superb views ahead and on both sides. At a junction of tracks bear left, and the track skirts woodland on the right to join a narrow lane **D**. Keep along it for nearly ¾ mile (1.2km), still along the ridge top and with conifer woodland to the right. Opposite a lane to Berwick St John on the left, turn right on to a broad, clear track **E**.

After passing through the narrow belt of conifers, the track descends steadily. Where it ends, keep straight ahead across a large field, making for the right edge of the trees in front. On reaching some gates, pass through, bearing slightly left with the track towards woodland. Continue gently downhill, skirting the right edge of Rotherley Wood. Soon the track passes through a hedge gap on the left; follow it to the right. Later, reach a field gate ahead, by an old contorted oak tree. Go through as waymarked, initially walking diagonally right on a grassy path.

Descend steeply, with lovely views of the valley ahead, to another metal gate, go through and continue along Tinkley

SCALE 1:25000 or 2½ INCHES to 1 MILE 4CM to 1KM

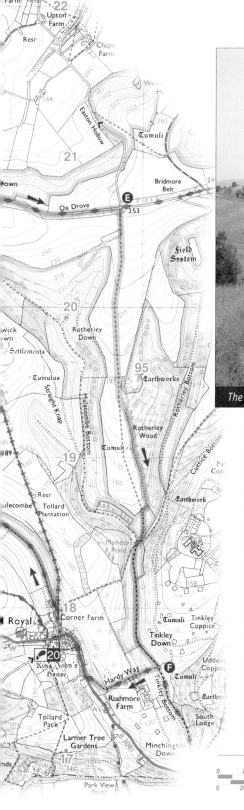

The ridge path on Win Green hill

Bottom, a delightful part of the
walk. Go through a metal gate,
and continue to the point where
there is a metal gate on the left
and one in front. Turn right **F**
and follow a faint path uphill
across grass to two gates ahead.
Pass through the left-hand one.
Walk ahead to a second gate,
pass alongside the fence and as
you continue over the brow of
the hill, the tower of Tollard
Royal church edges into view
over to the right.

Where the wire fence turns
right, continue along the track
which heads downhill and then
swings to the right. Go through a
metal gate on to a road and
follow it back to the start. ●

0	200	400	600	800 METRES	1
					KILOMETRES
					MILES
0	200	400	600 YARDS	½	

walk 21

Stonehenge

Start

Amesbury, Recreation Ground car park at the end of Recreation Road just across the bridge over the River Avon

Distance

7¾ miles (12.5km)

Height gain

575 feet (175m)

Approximate time

3¾ hours

Route terrain

Undulating paths and tracks lead from Amesbury to Stonehenge where the walk joins a National Trust permitted route

P Parking

Recreation Ground car park at Amesbury

OS maps

Landranger 184 (Salisbury & The Plain), Explorer 130 (Salisbury & Stonehenge)

GPS waypoints

SU 149 411
Ⓐ SU 144 402
Ⓑ SU 137 402
Ⓒ SU 134 398
Ⓓ SU 120 413
Ⓔ SU 120 423
Ⓕ SU 134 424
Ⓖ SU 137 428
Ⓗ SU 152 424

The highlight of this walk is the sudden view of Stonehenge ahead, dominating the skyline of Salisbury Plain and approached on foot across the downs, from where its location can be fully appreciated.

Amesbury is attractively situated on the River Avon which does a great loop to the south-west of the town. The church, with its Norman nave and 13th-century central tower, is unusually imposing. This is because it was probably the church of a medieval nunnery that stood nearby. After the dissolution of the monasteries in the 1530s, a house, Amesbury Abbey, was built on the site, and subsequently rebuilt in the 19th century. It is privately owned and not open to the public.

The walk begins just before the entrance to the Recreation Ground car park. Take the enclosed path which heads down to cross two footbridges, the first one over a stream and the second over the River Avon. Continue along a path which bears right to a crossroads of paths and a footpath post. Keep ahead, in the Durnford direction, along a steadily ascending, enclosed track. At a crossroads keep ahead over the crest of the hill and then descend gently, with fine views to the right over the

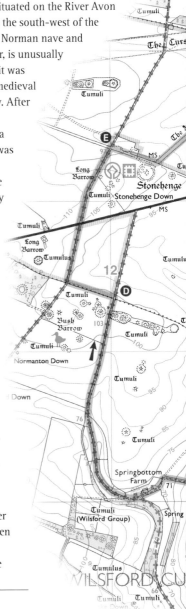

Avon Valley, to a dip. Turn right **Ⓐ**, as the track starts to climb and follow the path along the right edge of a field. In the field corner – near a chalk pit on the left – turn left along the bottom edge of the field, keep above a channel on the right, through a wooded area, then turn right over a footbridge. Continue along a winding path through trees – this part of the walk might be overgrown in the summer – and cross a footbridge over

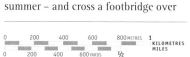

the Avon. Keep ahead over a ditch to a kissing-gate. Go through it and follow an enclosed path on to a lane in the hamlet of Normanton **B**.

Turn left, and just before reaching the medieval church at Wilsford, turn right **C** on to the tarmac drive to Springbottom Farm. After a few yards bear right off the drive and continue steadily uphill along a most attractive, tree-lined path. The path later descends gently and at the bottom bear left to rejoin the drive, which bears left and then curves gradually right, passing to the left of the farm buildings. It then continues as a rough track which peters out just before a fork. Continue along the right-hand, wide, grassy track which heads gently uphill towards the crest of the downs.

On reaching the crest, Stonehenge suddenly appears ahead in the distance, a stunning sight especially as the busy A303 is temporarily hidden from view. Pass between the Normanton Down Barrows, a series of Bronze Age burial chambers that stretches for over $\frac{1}{2}$ mile (800m) along the top of this low ridge, and shortly afterwards turn left at a gate **D**. Walk along the edge of a field, go through a gate in the field corner, and at a fingerpost turn right along a track to the main A303. Cross over this busy road *with great care*, keep along the track ahead to reach the visitor centre access lane to Stonehenge, formerly the A344, and turn right along it **E**.

Pass through a gate with National Trust signs and keep right along the field edge until you are level with the Heel Stone, a single block of sarsen stone. Bear left, following the line of The Avenue, built and used by early Bronze Age people, probably as a processional route to Stonehenge. The blue stones at the site might have been dragged along The Avenue on the last stage of their journey from Wales. The path's outline is visible, running through the grass. When you see a ladder-stile ahead, make for a gate and fence to the right of it and ascend the hillside, aiming for a gap between two bursts of woodland on the skyline. Head for a gate and turn left along the grassy track **F**.

Shortly after turning right you reach a T-junction **G**. Turn right, follow the track round a left bend and continue in a straight line for $\frac{3}{4}$ mile (1.2km), eventually reaching a road **H**. Turn right, use the underpass at a round-about into Amesbury and take the first turning on the right (High Street). Continue along Church Street, passing to the left of the church, and cross the River Avon. Where the road bends right, turn left, at a public footpath sign, along Recreation Road to the start. ●

Stonehenge

This is the most famous single prehistoric monument in Britain – possibly, indeed, in Europe. Mysteries abound and controversies rage about its purpose and construction, in particular why – and how – the smaller bluestones were brought all the way from the Preseli Hills in Pembrokeshire to be erected here. Although it looks deceptively simple, Stonehenge is a complex monument and appears to have been built in three main phases over a period of around 1,500 years. The first stage was the construction of a large circular bank and ditch around 3000BC. Next, about a thousand years later, came the circles of bluestones, which were subsequently re-arranged. Finally the circle of giant sarsen boulders with lintels, the most striking feature of the monument, was completed around 1400BC. Despite the crowds and the proximity of a busy main road, Stonehenge still manages to exert a powerful influence and one can only marvel at the engineering and organisational skills that were needed for its construction.

Great Bedwyn and Crofton Locks

Fields and forest take this walk to a pretty but isolated church and war memorial, before crossing the extensive parkland of Tottenham House. The return joins the summit section of the Kennet & Avon Canal as it emerges from the eastern portal of Bruce Tunnel. Of interest too is Crofton Pumping Station, built to lift the water used in the first flight of locks back to the top and, in Great Bedwyn, what must be the country's most unusually decorated post office.

walk 22

Start
Great Bedwyn, by the canal

Distance
8 miles (12.9km)

Height gain
445 feet (135m)

Approximate time
3¾ hours

Route terrain
Woodland and field paths, lane

P Parking
Car park at start

OS maps
Landranger 174 (Newbury & Wantage), Explorer 157 (Marlborough & Savernake Forest)

GPS waypoints
- SU 280 644
- Ⓐ SU 276 642
- Ⓑ SU 264 643
- Ⓒ SU 263 648
- Ⓓ SU 238 641
- Ⓔ SU 235 632

Out of the car park, go left over the canal bridge and walk up into the village. On reaching a small square, turn off left into Church Street. Carry on past the post office, decorated with a painted plasterwork Last Supper and medley of carved plaques and tombstones, and then the church, before leaving right up Shawgrove Ⓐ. Rounding the bend at the top, branch off right on a footpath and continue up between the fields behind. Keep going past Shawgrove Copse to a stile and carry

Kennet & Avon Canal Crofton Locks

Bruce Tunnel The Kennet & Avon Canal's summit pound runs for some 2½ miles (4km) between Brimslade Farm and Crofton Top Lock. The high point of the hill is at Wolfhall Bridge, and the original intention and cheapest option was to dig a deep cutting to accommodate the canal. However, the landowner, Thomas Brudenell-Bruce, objected and hence the canal was hidden within a tunnel. Nevertheless, the portal's inscription implies his enthusiasm, and only 50 years later the railway was allowed through in a cutting that actually bridges the canal.

on at the left field edge beyond. Passing behind a house in the subsequent field, look for a stile on the left **B**. Walk out beside the house boundary to its drive and go right, shortly joining the main forest drive. Eventually meeting another track, follow it right to a junction in front of some estate houses **C**.

Turn left and, ignoring side tracks, carry on through the trees for nearly ¾

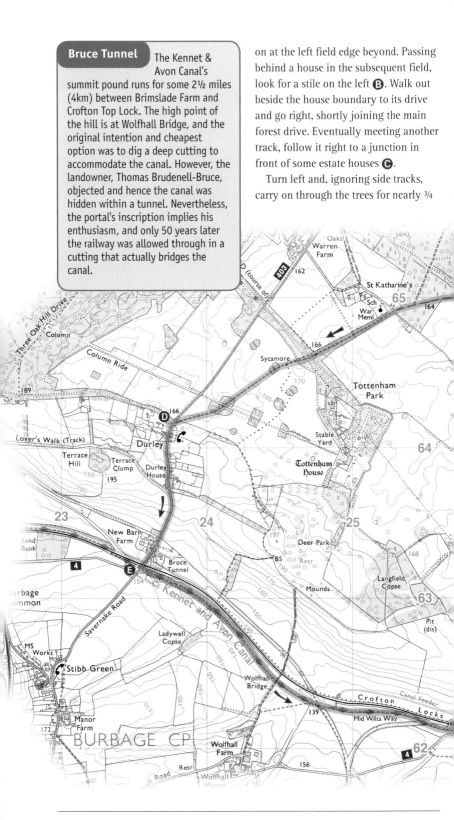

mile (1.2km) to a crossroads at the edge of the forest. Take the track ahead past St Katharine's Church and walk on within a long belt of trees. Ignore a crossing track and later, having passed through a gate, go over a drive and another track to emerge at the edge of open parkland. An ongoing trod guides the way past a lone sycamore and stand of beech towards more trees. Continue across another drive and past an old chalk pit, striking out across the rest of the park and ultimately leaving through a gate at the far side onto a lane **D**.

Go left through Durley and on down the hill. Approaching the bottom, a couple of bridges take you over, firstly

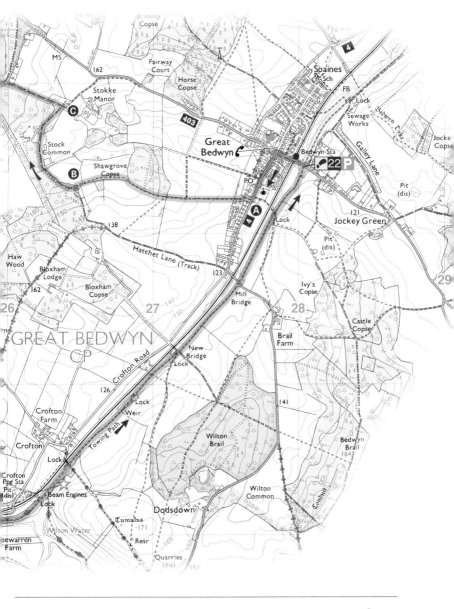

Crofton Pumping Station

Crofton Pumping Station

The summit sections of canals posed particular problems for their engineers in securing an adequate water supply. A broad lock, such as those on the Kennet & Avon, uses around 53,000 gallons for each boat passing through, and although that water goes on to feed the locks lower down the system, the top section needs replenishing. Reservoirs and surface water were used where possible, but occasionally a pumping station was necessary to lift water back up the hill. The Kennet & Avon has two, both restored to working order. That at Claverton near Bath is driven by a water wheel while the other, here at Crofton, is powered by steam. Water is taken from Wilton reservoir and lifted to feed back into the canal above the top lock.

the line of a disused railway and then, after a short way, the GWR Paddington–Exeter line. Of the canal, however, there is no sign, for it runs within Bruce Tunnel beneath your feet. So, immediately over the second bridge, turn off left on a drive signed as the Mid Wiltshire Way **E**. Just past the first house, branch off left on an enclosed path through trees, going left again a little further along down a flight of steps to reach the eastern portal of the tunnel. It is then a pleasant and easy canalside walk of some 3¾ miles (6km), dropping past a succession of ten locks and Crofton Pumping Station, which is open to the public, (and sometimes in steam on selected days) to return to Great Bedwyn. ●

Martinsell Hill and the Kennet & Avon Canal

walk 23

Start
Martinsell Hill

Distance
8 miles (12.9km)

Height gain
655 feet (200m)

Approximate time
4 hours

Route terrain
Field paths, towpath and lane

Parking
Car park at start

OS maps
Landranger 173 (Swindon & Devizes), Explorer 157 (Marlborough & Savernake Forest)

GPS waypoints

- SU 183 645
- Ⓐ SU 175 636
- Ⓑ SU 165 632
- Ⓒ SU 161 628
- Ⓓ SU 163 615
- Ⓔ SU 164 611
- Ⓕ SU 198 629
- Ⓖ SU 199 642

On a really clear day, it should be possible to see the Isle of Wight, some 40 miles (65km) away from the top of Martinsell Hill, but even closer views across the Vale of Pewsey are expansive. Additional highlights include a wetland nature reserve, a pleasant section by the Kennet and Avon Canal, and a handy pub offering refreshment before the steady pull back onto the down in the latter stages of the walk.

Through a gate at the back of the car park, head away on a grass trail that curves gently across the slope of the hill towards trees. Approaching the trees, fork left, continuing up between them. Breaking out at the far side, swing left with a fence on your right and carry on along the edge of the escarpment. Later pass through scrub and some curiously shaped pines to reach a stile at the far end of the trees leading onto grassland Ⓐ. Walk on by a fence on the left, now gently losing height. Passing through a gate at the foot of the enclosure, keep going along a broad descending ridge towards Giant's Grave, which can be seen ahead. Go through an

Martinsell Hill

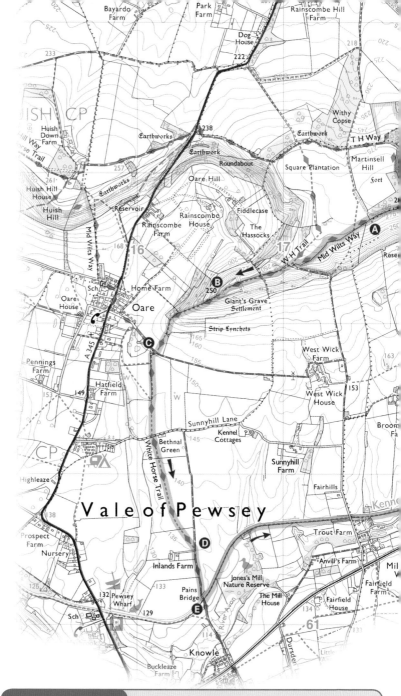

Iron Age Enclosures   There is a large Iron Age fort on the top of Martinsell Hill, although being screened by trees, it is hardly visible from the walk. However, further on as the route descends a long promontory ridge, there is a smaller settlement enclosure known as Giant's Grave. A single but impressive bank and ditch separates it from the higher part of the ridge, where there is a second although less prominent earthwork. Towards the bottom of the hill on its southern flank are a number of medieval cultivation lynchets.

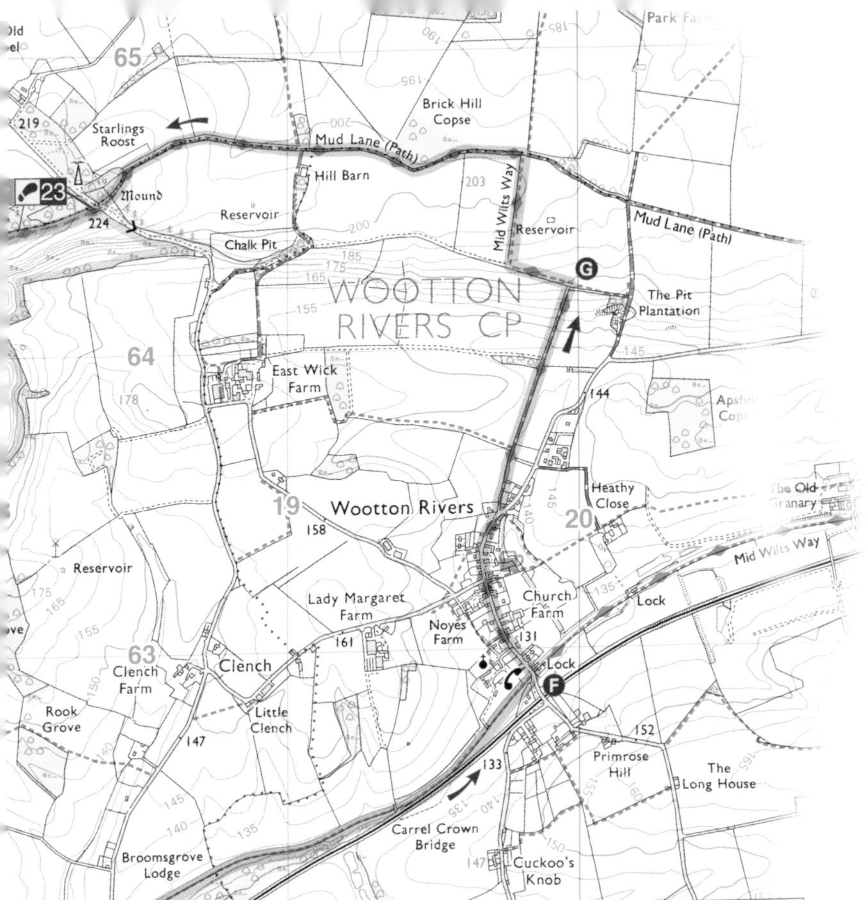

The map shows an area with labels including:

65 · Park Farm · Brick Hill Copse · Starlings Roost · Mud Lane (Path) · 219 · Mound · 23 · Hill Barn · 203 · Mid Wilts Way · Reservoir · Mud Lane (Path) · 224 · Chalk Pit · Reservoir · G · The Pit Plantation · WOOTTON RIVERS CP · 155 · 145 · 64 · East Wick Farm · 178 · 144 · Apsh... Cop... · The Old Granary · 19 · Wootton Rivers · 158 · Heathy Close · 20 · Mid Wilts Way · Reservoir · Lady Margaret Farm · 135 · 161 · Noyes Farm · Church Farm · Lock · 63 · Clench Farm · Clench · 131 · Lock · F · Rook Grove · Little Clench · 147 · 152 · 133 · Primrose Hill · The Long House · 145 · 140 · 135 · Broomsgrove Lodge · Carrel Crown Bridge · 147 · Cuckoo's Knob · ...von Canal · 62 · Totteridge Farm · 4 · New Mill · Deane Water · MILTON LILBOURNE C... · 138 · 138 · Littleworth

SCALE 1:25000 or 2½ INCHES to 1 MILE 4CM to 1KM

0 200 400 600 800 METRES 1 KILOMETRES MILES
0 200 400 600 YARDS ½

intervening gate to pass the trig column, which stands on the other side of the fence **B**.

Beyond Giant's Grave, the ongoing path drops steeply off the hill towards Oare. The large building seen in the village below is Oare House, built in 1740 for Henry Deacon, a London wine merchant. The splendid gardens are

Dropping from Giant's Grave

Bridge 110 on the Kennet & Avon Canal

opened to the public twice a year under the National Garden Scheme. At the bottom, pass through a gate in a tangle of trees. Cross a field to a small gate near the far left corner to emerge onto a track **C**.

Cross to the grass field track opposite and walk away with the hedge on your right. Meeting a lane, cross to the footpath opposite and continue across a couple of fields. Entering a third field, bear left across the corner, coming out onto a farm lane **D**. Follow it right, keeping ahead on a grass track where it subsequently turns into Inlands Farm to reach Pains Bridge across the Kennet & Avon Canal **E**. Cross the bridge and drop left to the towpath, beside which is an access gate to Jones's Mill, the Vera Jean's Nature Reserve.

Follow the canal away from the bridge for some 2½ miles (4km) until bridge No. 108 at Wootton Rivers **F**. Climb to the lane and turn over the bridge to walk up through the village,

shortly passing **The Royal Oak**. Carry on for a further 250 yards and then branch off left on a rising track. A bit of a pull at the top takes the track into a field **G**. Turn left along its edge. In the corner go right and stay by the left hedge over the crest of the hill, falling to a gap at the far side. Pass through onto a wooded track and go left. A mile's walking (1.6km) brings you out on a lane opposite the car park.

Wootton Rivers

Today a sleepy village of attractive thatched cottages with only a church and pub, Wootton Rivers once had an iron foundry and agricultural machinery factory. St Andrew's is an appealing building with a wooden bell turret perched above the gable with an unusual clock face bearing the letters G L O R Y B E T O G O D. It was made to celebrate the coronation of George V in 1911 and plays tunes rather than chime the hours.

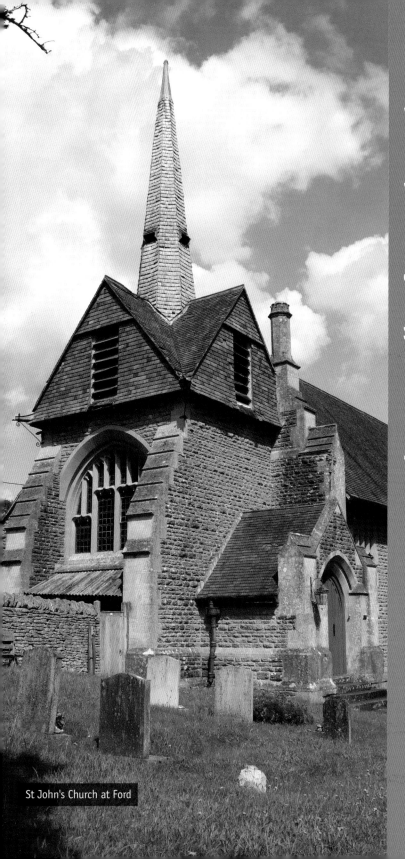

St John's Church at Ford

walk 24

Castle Combe

Start
Upper Castle Coombe

Distance
8½ miles (13.7km)

Height gain
850 feet (260m)

Approximate time
4¼ hours

Route terrain
Field and woodland paths, some lane

Parking
Car park at start

OS maps
Landranger 173 (Swindon & Devizes), Explorer 156 (Chippenham & Bradford-on-Avon)

GPS waypoints
- ST 845 777
- **A** ST 840 768
- **B** ST 850 756
- **C** ST 845 750
- **D** ST 822 747
- **E** ST 817 756
- **F** ST 813 771
- **G** ST 824 770
- **H** ST 833 775

An impressively lovely walk beginning from one of England's prettiest villages, it loosely follows the wooded valleys of three separate streams and 'completes the circle' over undulating upland fields. Among the many things of interest in the village at the start are the ancient church, a covered market cross and a 500-year-old pub.

Leave the car park and follow the lane towards the lower village. Bear right at a junction and continue downhill to the square and covered market cross at the old heart of Castle Combe. Bear left through the village, shortly crossing a bridge over By Brook. Keep going, now beside the stream. Carry on past a private bridge giving access to Brook House to reach a second bridge, just a little farther along **A**.

Abandon the lane there, crossing the stream onto a clear path that rises to contour the sloping meadows and trees of the valley side. Eventually entering woodland, ignore a waymarked path off right and remain with the ongoing track. Farther on, beyond a couple of consecutive gates, the trail eventually breaks from the trees to drop past Upper Long Dean Mill, where it becomes a lane.

As the lane swings left **B**, bear off right and then fork right to remain with the bridleway. Carry on over a bridge and past a house, the track now climbing along a narrow wooded ridge. Through a gate at the top, the way leaves the trees to run above a sloping meadow from which there is a fine view along the valley. Where the contained bridleway shortly bends right, pass through a kissing-gate and follow a trod across the meadow towards trees at the far side.

Emerge through a final kissing-gate onto a lane **C** and turn downhill to reach the main road at the bottom. Go right for 250 yards, passing the slender wooden spire of St John's Church to then immediately turn off up a narrow lane, the Old Coach Road.

It is a bit of a climb to the top, but

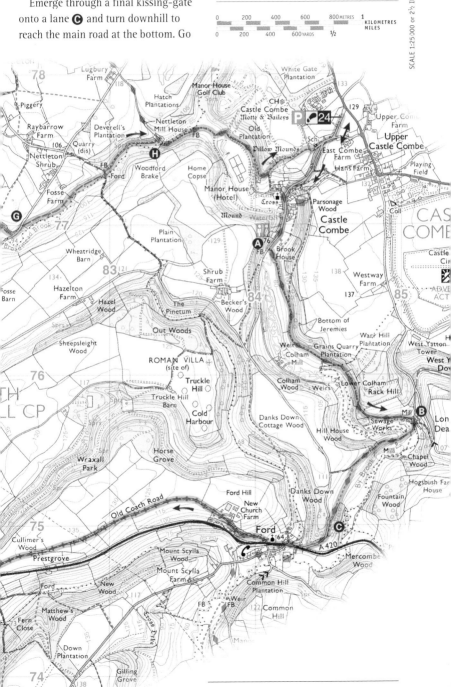

beyond New Church Farm the gradient eases and the way continues as a pleasant track above the Doncombe Valley. Meeting a lane at the far end **(D)**, walk right and follow it steeply down into a valley and up the other side into North Wraxall. Towards the top, keep left past the church and go right at the junction just beyond. The lane rises over the crest of the hill past Court Close Farm, shortly passing beneath pylon cables. Immediately, turn off over a stile on the left **(E)** and bear right across a field to a gate and stile on the opposite side.

There, emerging onto a narrow lane, cross to the gate opposite. Go right and left within the field corner, walking on a further few yards to find a stile on the right. Turn left in the adjacent field and head down into a deep dip before climbing to a stile in the top fence out onto another narrow lane.

Cross to the field opposite and stride on with a wall on your left. After 200 yards, slip through a gap and continue on the opposite side of the boundary. Keep going at the edge of successive fields, the way developing as a track and ultimately joining the end of a lane at the edge of West Kington. As the lane then bends left past houses, keep ahead on a marked bridleway next to the end cottage garden. Ignore a crossing track and carry on beside a field before dropping out at the bottom onto a lane **(F)**. Go right above Parsonage Wood.

After 150 yards, reaching the end of a wall, branch off left on a bridleway. Wind down to cross Broadmead Brook and head downstream on the opposite bank. Beyond a couple of small meadows, the way continues as a track across the slope of a grass bank. Where it later curves up to a gate, bear off to stay with the lower meadow. At the far end, bend left in front of a gate to exit

through a second gate just beyond onto a lane. Follow it left up the hill.

As the gradient eases, look for a path departing through a bridle gate on the right **(G)**. The trail drops through trees and scrub, breaking out to continue along the valley. The way remains clear, alternating between meadows and woodland and passing through occasional gates before eventually falling to the stream by a ford and clapper bridge. However, remain on this bank, but as the path then turns from the stream, abandon it through a gate on the right. Carry on along the wooded valley, in time emerging onto at track at Nettleton Mill **(H)**. Go right to find a path leaving through a kissing-gate in the high wall at the end. Wind across the brook and continue downstream through woodland.

Before long, the path approaches Manor House Golf Course, and there is a bell beside the path for you to warn golfers of your presence. Keeping a wary eye open for flying golf balls, walk out onto the course and follow a tarmac path to the right, shortly re-crossing the stream on an elegant stone bridge. Immediately, turn off right, but after only a few yards, bear left through rough grass and scrub on a path rising gently along the valley side. After passing into trees, it runs in front of a wall to a gate, from which a path drops into the old village centre. However, the way back is to the left, climbing on beside the wall. Emerging from the trees, walk on briefly at the edge of another section of the golf course before curving away right into scrub. The way continues beside a paddock and then comes out onto a drive. Walk ahead past cottages to meet a lane and follow it up left, branching left again at a junction to return to the car park. ●

Barbury Castle and Ogbourne St Andrew

walk 25

From the superb viewpoint of Barbury Castle, a prehistoric hill-fort high up on the Marlborough Downs, the route follows the Ridgeway down into the valley of the little River Og to the village of Ogbourne St Andrew. From here tracks lead back on to the open downs for an invigorating final stretch back to the fort. There are clear, broad tracks all the way, the views are extensive and all the gradients are gradual.

The walk begins on the Ridgeway – possibly the oldest routeway in Britain – which runs along the south side of the car park. *Although the main part of the route lies to the left, first turn right, passing an information centre and going through a gate, to visit the earthworks of Barbury Castle, a large Iron Age fort defended by a double bank and ditches.* The ditches enclose an area of $12\frac{1}{2}$ acres (5 ha), and the site may have been re-fortified in Saxon times, as excavations have revealed evidence of a long period of occupation. As well as being impressive in its own right, the fort is also a magnificent viewpoint.

Retrace your steps to the car park and continue along the Ridgeway to a gateway. Go through and turn right along a track. At a Ridgeway post turn left **A** to follow a track across

Start
Barbury Castle Country Park, signposted from B4005 to the east of Chiseldon

Distance
9 miles (14.5km)

Height gain
755 feet (230m)

Approximate time
4½ hours

Route terrain
Exposed downland; undulating bridleways and byways

Parking
Barbury Castle Country Park

OS maps
Landranger 173 (Swindon & Devizes), Explorer 157 (Marlborough & Savernake Forest)

GPS waypoints

SU 156 760
A SU 158 758
B SU 192 746
C SU 188 722
D SU 177 728
E SU 167 731

Marlborough Downs

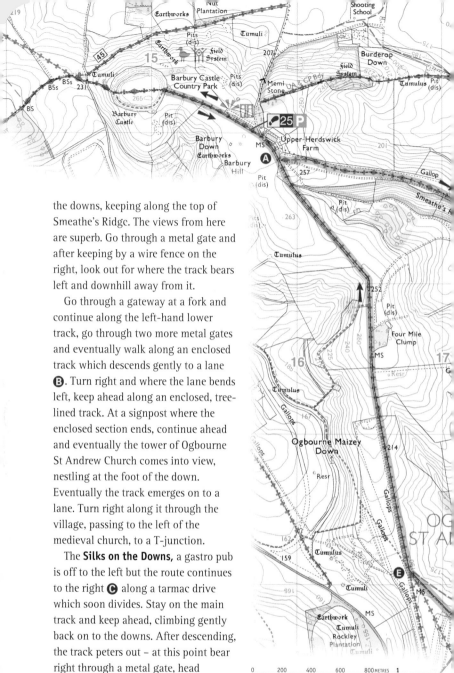

the downs, keeping along the top of Smeathe's Ridge. The views from here are superb. Go through a metal gate and after keeping by a wire fence on the right, look out for where the track bears left and downhill away from it.

Go through a gateway at a fork and continue along the left-hand lower track, go through two more metal gates and eventually walk along an enclosed track which descends gently to a lane **B**. Turn right and where the lane bends left, keep ahead along an enclosed, tree-lined track. At a signpost where the enclosed section ends, continue ahead and eventually the tower of Ogbourne St Andrew Church comes into view, nestling at the foot of the down. Eventually the track emerges on to a lane. Turn right along it through the village, passing to the left of the medieval church, to a T-junction.

The **Silks on the Downs,** a gastro pub is off to the left but the route continues to the right **C** along a tarmac drive which soon divides. Stay on the main track and keep ahead, climbing gently back on to the downs. After descending, the track peters out – at this point bear right through a metal gate, head downhill across a field and in the bottom corner go through another metal gate on to a track **D**. Turn left and the track bends right and heads uphill towards a large barn on the skyline.

Pass to the right of this barn and turn right along a track. On joining a broader track at a Byway sign, bear right along it **E** and follow it gently uphill across the broad downs. The track continues along the left inside edge of a group of trees, Four Mile Clump, and leads back to the start.

walk 26

Savernake Forest

Start

Marlborough

Distance

8¾ miles (14.1km)

Height gain

705 feet (215m)

Approximate time

4½ hours

Route terrain

Forest paths and tracks and a stretch of disused railway

Parking

Pay and Display car park at Marlborough

OS maps

Landranger 73 (Swindon & Devizes) and 174 (Newbury & Wantage), Explorer 157 (Marlborough & Savernake Forest)

GPS waypoints

- SU 188 692
- Ⓐ SU 192 694
- Ⓑ SU 201 693
- Ⓒ SU 214 697
- Ⓓ SU 214 691
- Ⓔ SU 218 682
- Ⓕ SU 224 679
- Ⓖ SU 225 667
- Ⓗ SU 208 667
- Ⓙ SU 208 675
- Ⓚ SU 198 686

The first part of this highly attractive walk is along the Kennet valley to the east of Marlborough, between the Marlborough Downs and Savernake Forest. Most of the remainder is through the extensive woodlands and glades of the forest, survivals of an ancient royal hunting ground that once covered much of eastern Wiltshire. Although a lengthy walk, it is not particularly strenuous and there are no steep gradients, but expect some muddy footpaths in places. There is no right of access in Savernake Forest. However, the public may use it throughout the year, though they are asked to respect the few signs protecting the various groups of private houses on the estate.

Grand Avenue in autumn, Savernake Forest

Marlborough's long, unusually wide and handsome High Street reflects the town's importance throughout the centuries as a staging post on the main road from London to Bath and Bristol. A church stands at each end of it – at the west end is the 15th-century St Peter's and beyond that the buildings of Marlborough College. At the east end behind the Town Hall is St Mary's, mostly rebuilt in the Cromwellian period following the Great Fire of 1653 which destroyed much of the town and gutted the church, though it does retain a fine Norman doorway at the west end.

The walk starts at the east end of the High Street in front of the Town Hall, which was built between 1900 and 1902 on the site of its predecessor. Pass to the left of the Town Hall and follow the road to the left, then take the first turning on the right (Silverless Street). Keep ahead at a crossroads by The Green, site of the original Saxon settlement of Marlborough, and continue along the road for 270 yards turning right after a row of houses into Stonebridge Lane **A**. Follow this path downhill and cross the footbridge over the River Kennet. Turn sharp left onto a path and continue as it meanders through fields before veering left at a fork. Cross the river again by a wooden footbridge and turn right to pick up a footpath through the field.

Head across to the right-hand corner of the field and go through a metal gate into woodland, climb a stile, ascend steps, cross a disused railway track **B** and descend steps on the other side. Follow the path along the right edge of a field, and at a corner turn right on to a track. The track soon curves left and continues along the right edge of fields. Go through a kissing-gate just to the left of a field corner, at a public footpath sign and continue along a track

between farm buildings. Turn left on to a tarmac drive, immediately turn right and after a few yards turn left up steps and go through a lychgate into Mildenhall (shortened locally to Minal) churchyard. Pass to the right of the church, a most attractive and interesting building which retains an impressive Norman nave and was extensively remodelled in the Georgian period.

Follow the path to the left and bear right to go through two kissing-gates in quick succession. Walk across a field, keeping parallel to a wire fence on the right, go through a gate, and then keep over to the right-hand side of the field alongside a fence. Go through a metal gate, walk along the right edge of a cricket field and in the corner keep ahead along an enclosed path to a lane **C**.

Turn right, cross the River Kennet, then follow the narrow lane round right-and left-hand bends and head up to a T-junction. Turn left and at a fork ahead, take the right-hand, tarmac drive **D**. After passing in front of a bungalow, the drive becomes a rough track which heads uphill through trees. Cross a track, continue up to cross another and take the narrow, tree-lined path ahead (Cock-a-troop Lane) – this may be overgrown in places – then enter Savernake Forest.

Originally a royal forest, in the 16th century Savernake passed into the ownership of the powerful Seymour family – it was here that Henry VIII courted his third wife, Jane Seymour – and at the end of the 17th century passed to the Bruces, later earls of Ailesbury. It is still owned by that family, but most of it is leased to the Forestry Commission. Savernake is noted for its avenues, particularly the Grand Avenue, a great beech-lined drive planted by the third Earl of

Ailesbury in the 18th century.

Keep ahead to a public footpath sign and turn left along a track **E**. Pass beside a barrier and continue through a beautiful stretch of woodland, descending slightly to a lane. Turn right along it to the A4, turn right and after a few yards turn sharp left **F** along a straight forest track. Go down the slope, pass a circular parking-and-turning area on the right under some beech trees and after about 30 yards, veer half right at a barrier, following a straight track up a gentle slope. Pass through extensive woodland to reach fields bordering the track. Continue ahead to a barrier beyond which is the junction for Eight Walks. Take the second right exit **G** (no through road) and where it bends left after nearly 1 mile (1.6km), keep ahead along a rough track. About 100 yards before reaching a road, keep a sharp lookout for a right turn into the woods **H**. Descend gently along the woodland path (Church Walk). At the bottom keep right at a fork, very briefly, before bearing left across an open grassy area to pass round the right-hand edge of a sizeable fallen tree, winding round to the left and then to the right on a track that becomes gradually more established as it passes through woodland. Keep ahead on a broad grassy path, continue ahead at the first crossroads and descend to a junction with a track. Here turn left **J** and follow the track (Long Harry) through the trees, eventually reaching a track and then a barrier immediately beyond it. Continue to Postern Hill picnic site and when the track bends left (just beyond a sign Barbecue Hearth – bookable area), take the right-hand fork. Pass a sign 'Site 6' and then bend right at the next junction. Keep along the right edge of an open area of grassland, follow it round to the right

SCALE 1:25000 or 2½ INCHES to 1 MILE 4CM to 1KM

by a sign for Site 3 and follow the broad path through trees. Cross over a path and descend with views of Marlborough to reach the former Chiseldon and Marlborough railway, now a designated walking and cycling route. Turn right **K**.

Walk along the hedge-lined track which, after passing under a bridge, curves gradually left. The next section is beautifully tree-lined and there is a dramatic view as you cross a bridge high above the River Kennet. Continue through woodland and look out for wooden rails and steps on both sides of the track. Here turn left **B** down the steps, rejoining the outward route, and retrace your steps into Marlborough and the starting point of the walk. ●

Cherhill White Horse and Windmill Hill

Start
Roadside lay-by beside A4, ¾ mile (1.2km) west of Beckhampton roundabout

Distance
9¼ miles (14.9km)

Height gain
855 feet (260m)

Approximate time
4¾ hours

Route terrain
Field paths, tracks and lane

Parking
Roadside lay-by

OS maps
Landranger 173 (Swindon & Devizes), Explorer 157 (Marlborough & Savernake Forest)

GPS waypoints
　SU 076 692
Ⓐ SU 055 699
Ⓑ SU 051 692
Ⓒ SU 040 700
Ⓓ SU 057 715
Ⓔ SU 066 714
Ⓕ SU 079 720
Ⓖ SU 086 713
Ⓗ SU 071 697

Those attracted to the 'sport of kings' may get no further than the car park, which overlooks an extensive gallops, where racehorses can often be seen being put through their paces in the early morning. But stride on, for there is much more to see along the way, in earthworks, tumuli and Iron Age fortifications. The ramble also features an impressive monument and white horse on Cherhill Hill and for those wishing to go the extra mile, there's a pub en route too.

Begin through a bridle gate at the far end of the lay-by. Take the left branch of parallel paths that climb onto Knoll Down, from where there is a view across to the Lansdowne Monument on Cherhill Hill. Ignore a path coming in from the right and carry on ahead along the line of the Old Bath Road. Later on, the path and a parallel bridleway combine, passing a tumulus to reach a T-junction Ⓐ.

Turn left, climbing to a barn and small covered reservoir. Where the track then splits, keep right through a gate and continue climbing onto Cherhill Down, eventually reaching a junction by the eastern entrance of Oldbury Castle Ⓑ.

Cherhill Hill　Looking back from the main road, it is possible to see all three of the historic monuments on Cherhill Hill. Perhaps the most prominent, and a landmark for miles around, is the Lansdowne Monument, a 125-foot (38-m) high obelisk erected in 1845 by the third Marquis of Lansdowne to celebrate his great-great-grandfather, Sir William Petty. Petty had a wide ranging interest that covered medicine, surveying, politics, economics, philosophy and science, and was a member of the Royal Society. The Cherhill White Horse, high on the slope to the east was cut in 1780 under the direction of Dr Christopher Alsop, coincidentally a friend of the Liverpool artist George Stubbs who specialised in painting animals, particularly horses. The third of the hill's monuments is the impressive Oldbury Castle, an extensive bivallate (double bank and ditch) Iron Age fort. It was occupied from around 500BC until the arrival of the Romans and surrounded an earlier enclosure settled towards the end of the Bronze Age.

Cherhill from the Old Bath Road

Go right, winding through the defensive gateway and continuing to the Lansdowne Monument at the far side of the earthwork-enclosed area. Pass on the left, the path then descending. Keep left at a fork down to a gate, and then branch off right on a path to the top of a satellite summit, from which there is a view out right to the Cherhill White Horse. Drop down on the other side to gates at the bottom. Ignore the first gate on the right and carry on round the corner of the fence to a second. Turn through that and go left along a sunken path leading off the hill to the main road at the edge of the village of Cherhill **C**.

The **Black Horse** lies a little over ¼ mile (400m) to the left, but the onward route lies along Park Lane opposite. Climb up at the edge of the village, past a junction with The Street, but branch off right beyond along a signed byway. After later passing a bridleway joining

from the left, watch for a wartime pillbox in the field on the right. Farther on, largely hidden by trees are the surviving buildings of the West Camp of RAF Yatesbury. Carry on until you meet a lane at the end of the track **D**.

Turn right to a junction and then left along The Avenue. Farther on, a lane off left leads to All Saints' Church where there are a number of War Graves containing personnel who died while serving at RAF Yatesbury. Return and walk on along the main lane to a junction by a bus shelter **E**. Go right to Yatesbury House Farm and continue past Little London on a track. Soon reaching a junction, turn left to pass through Snake's Lane Plantation and on to the top of a shallow hill where there are several gates **F**. Take the bridle gate on the right and follow a path through a long belt of trees. Emerging at the far end onto a crossing track, the gate opposite opens onto Windmill Hill;

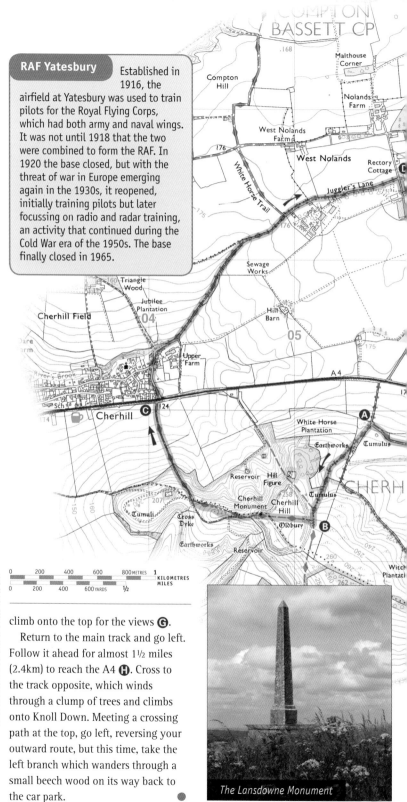

RAF Yatesbury Established in 1916, the airfield at Yatesbury was used to train pilots for the Royal Flying Corps, which had both army and naval wings. It was not until 1918 that the two were combined to form the RAF. In 1920 the base closed, but with the threat of war in Europe emerging again in the 1930s, it reopened, initially training pilots but later focussing on radio and radar training, an activity that continued during the Cold War era of the 1950s. The base finally closed in 1965.

SCALE 1:25000 or 2½ INCHES to 1 MILE 4CM to 1KM

climb onto the top for the views **G**.

Return to the main track and go left. Follow it ahead for almost 1½ miles (2.4km) to reach the A4 **H**. Cross to the track opposite, which winds through a clump of trees and climbs onto Knoll Down. Meeting a crossing path at the top, go left, reversing your outward route, but this time, take the left branch which wanders through a small beech wood on its way back to the car park.

The Lansdowne Monument

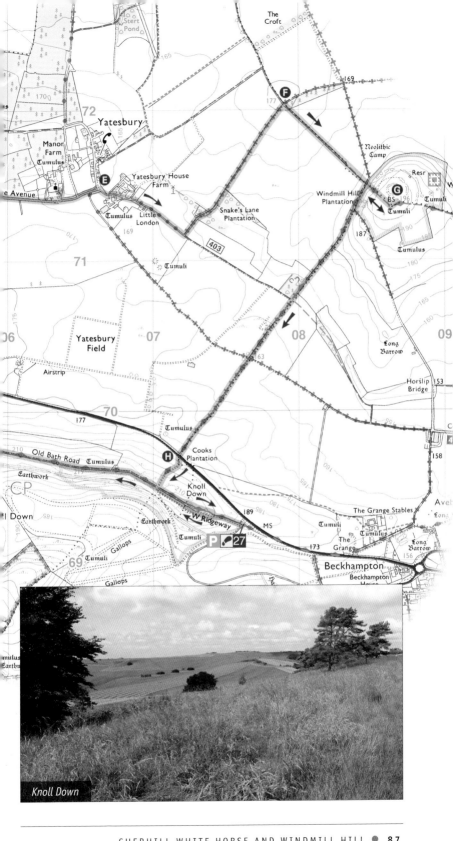

Knoll Down

walk 28

Cold Kitchen Hill and Shear Water

Start

Shear Water

Distance

10 miles (16.1km)

Height gain

1,100 feet (335m)

Approximate time

5 hours

Route terrain

Downland paths and track, woodland and lane

Parking

Shear Water car park

OS maps

Landranger 183 (Yeovil & Frome), Explorer 143 (Warminster & Trowbridge)

GPS waypoints

- ST 854 420
- Ⓐ ST 851 417
- Ⓑ ST 860 389
- Ⓒ ST 853 391
- Ⓓ ST 846 383
- Ⓔ ST 827 391
- Ⓕ ST 826 409
- Ⓖ ST 841 413
- Ⓗ ST 838 419

Beginning at the edge of Longleat Forest, this is a walk of wonderful contrasts between open downland and dense woodland, initially heading towards the chalk hills that rise prominently to the south. The way avoids the obvious route over Brims Down, instead taking a more scenic way past Woodcombe Farm to regain the hill from the south. A gently undulating route runs over Cold Kitchen Hill onto Whitecliff Down, from which there are superb views. The ongoing ramble falls away through woodland and open farmland to finish with a pleasant stroll through the forest and round the northern edge of the man-made Shear Water lake.

Leave the rear of the car park beside a barrier at its northern end and follow a track rising into the trees. At a junction, keep with the climbing path ahead, but after the gradient eases higher up, watch for a faint track leaving sharp right. It soon settles beside the top boundary of the plantation. Reaching a corner Ⓐ, turn left out of the trees and follow a gently falling track, tree-lined to the right and open fields on the left.

Meeting a crossways, go right and then left to continue on a downhill track, which ends at a lane. Turn right, but a few yards on, just before the entrance to Wing Farm, take a path off on the left. Shortly, go over a crossing bridleway and keep ahead on a hedged track that begins to climb. It eventually leads to a field gate and crossing track at the top.

To the left, it heads down the hill to Woodcombe Farm. At the junction there with its access drive Ⓑ, go right past barns and follow the ongoing track to climb back onto Brims Down. After an initial steep pull, the way settles into a gradual climb across sloping chalk grassland. Reaching the crest of the hill, a sign marks a crossing bridleway Ⓒ. Follow it to the left, shortly passing through a double field gate. Wind left and then right with the ongoing trail, and carry on to reach a junction of gated tracks by a large building.

Stick with the waymarked bridleway opposite, which climbs on past a large barrow onto the top of Cold Kitchen Hill, marked by a trig column just to the left Ⓓ. It is a grand spot from which to enjoy far-reaching views and you may hear the call of ravens too. Large, black birds with a heavy beak; they are the largest members of the crow family.

Keep with the ongoing track, descending to meet the Mid

Wilts Way, which runs along the bottom boundary of the field. Follow it right past a beacon post and on at the edge of the next field, where the ground begins to rise onto Whitecliff Down. Passing into yet another field, keep by the left fence.

Approaching the top, curve round to the right into a narrowing extension of the field and pick up a bridleway through a gate over on the left into the trees, marked the Mid Wilts Way **E**. The trail soon drops steeply through the trees, eventually emerging at the bottom edge of the wood. Ignore the byway signed off right and carry on with the path ahead down the hill, which ultimately leads out onto a lane.

Go left, but then almost immediately turn off right along a pleasant, hedged track, which in time leads through to a second lane **F**. Walk right past Parsonage Farm. Shortly, at a sharp bend, leave though a gate gap ahead. Stroll on by the right-hand field edge, passing a trig pillar half-way along. Exit through a gate at the bottom corner onto another lane by Lower Shutes Cottage. Follow it to the left for ¼ mile (400m), taking care, especially if walking with children or dogs, for the lane can be busy.

Just after the entrance to Shute Farm (on the right), watch for a track off left beside a barrier into Manswood **G**. Where it almost immediately forks, bear right on a lesser path and walk parallel to the road. Reaching a good track from

Woodcombe Bottom

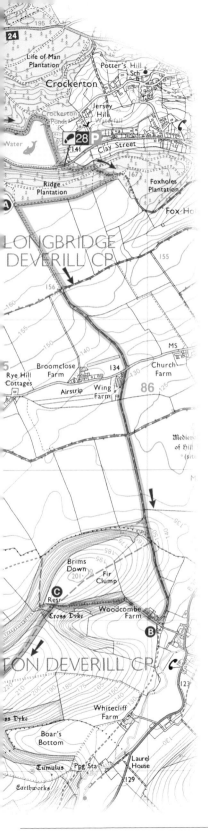

Keep a look-out Apart from the splendid views, there is much to see on this grand walk. In the sky, look out for buzzard and raven (unmistakable for their size), while on the ground there may be partridge and pheasant. Hare and deer might sometimes be seen, and at the right time of year, there are bluebells and poppies. The hills to the south-west of Crockerton have been inhabited since the Stone Age and, on the south flank along the Wylye valley, there are several groups of earthworks, while near the top of Cold Kitchen Hill is a long barrow that is perhaps 5,500 years old.

behind Swancombe Cottage, bear left and follow it for about ½ mile (800m), keeping a lookout in season for speckled wood butterflies and magnificent emperor dragonflies hawking the rides. Reaching a junction **H**, turn sharp right, in time approaching Shear Water, hidden behind the trees. The way curves round above the end of the lake, shortly dipping across a stream. At a junction just beyond, keep right to reach and follow the water's northern edge. The path eventually leads round to cross the dam that holds the lake back above Crockerton Ponds. Walk out to the road, passing a tea room, to find the car park opposite. ●

Longleat Part of the Longleat estate, Shear Water lake was created towards the end of the 18th century by damming a small stream. It is the largest in a series along the valley and is regarded as one of the finest fishing lakes in the country. The Elizabethan manor of Longleat House, its gardens and safari park are situated some 2½ miles (4km) to the west. The estate has been the seat of the Thynne family since 1541, having previously been an Augustinian priory.

Further Information

Walking Safety

Although the reasonably gentle countryside that is the subject of this book offers no real dangers to walkers at any time of the year, it is still advisable to take sensible precautions and follow certain well-tried guidelines.

Always take with you both warm and waterproof clothing and sufficient food and drink. Wear suitable footwear, such as strong walking boots or shoes that give a good grip over stony ground, on slippery slopes and in muddy conditions. Try to obtain a local weather forecast and bear it in mind before you start. Do not be afraid to abandon your proposed route and return to your starting point in the event of a sudden and unexpected deterioration in the weather.

All the walks described in this book will be safe to do, given due care and respect, even during the winter. Indeed, a crisp, fine winter day often provides perfect walking conditions, with firm ground underfoot and a clarity unique to this time of the year. The most difficult hazard likely to be encountered is mud, especially when walking along woodland and field paths, farm tracks and bridleways – the latter in particular can often get churned up by cyclists and horses. In summer, an additional difficulty may be narrow and overgrown paths, particularly along the edges of cultivated fields. Always ensure appropriate footwear is worn.

Walkers and the Law

The Countryside and Rights of Way Act (CRoW Act 2000) gives a public right of access in England and Wales to land mapped as open country (mountain, moor, heath and down) or registered common land. These areas are known as *open access land*, and include land around the coastline, known as *coastal margins*.

Where You Can Go
Rights of Way

Prior to the introduction of the CRoW Act, walkers could only legally access the countryside along public rights of way. These are either 'footpaths' (for walkers only) or 'bridleways' (for walkers, riders on horseback and pedal cyclists). A third category called 'Byways open to all traffic' (BOATs), is used by motorised vehicles as well as those using non-mechanised transport. Mainly they are green lanes, farm and estate roads, although occasionally they will be found crossing mountainous area.

Rights of way are marked on Ordnance Survey maps. Look for the green broken lines on the Explorer maps, or the red dashed lines on Landranger maps.

The term 'right of way' means exactly what it says. It gives a right of passage over what, for the most part, is private land. Under pre-CRoW legislation walkers were required to keep to the line of the right of way and not stray onto land on either side. If you did inadvertently wander off the right of way, either because of faulty map reading or because the route was not clearly indicated on the ground, you were technically trespassing.

Local authorities have a legal obligation to ensure that rights of way are kept clear and free of obstruction, and are signposted where they leave metalled roads. The duty of local authorities to install signposts extends to the placing of signs along a path or way, but only where the authority considers it necessary to have a signpost or waymark to assist persons unfamiliar with the locality.

CRoW Access Rights
Access Land

As well as being able to walk on existing rights of way, under CRoW legislation you have access to large areas of open land and, under further legislation, a right of coastal access, which is being implemented by Natural England, giving for the first time the right of access around all England's open coast. This includes plans for an England Coast Path (ECP) which will run for 2,795 miles (4,500 kilometres). A corresponding Wales Coast Path has been open since 2012.

Coastal access rights apply within the coastal margin (including along the ECP) unless the land falls into a category of excepted land or is subject to local restrictions, exclusions or diversions.

You can of course continue to use rights of way to cross access land, but you can lawfully leave the path and wander at will in these designated areas.

Where to Walk
Access Land is shown on Ordnance Survey Explorer maps by a light yellow tint surrounded by a pale orange border. New orange coloured 'i' symbols on the maps will show the location of permanent access information boards installed by the access authorities. Coastal Margin is shown on Ordnance Survey Explorer maps by a pink tint.

Restrictions
The right to walk on access land may lawfully be restricted by landowners, but whatever restrictions are put into place on access land they have no effect on existing rights of way, and you can continue to walk on them.

Dogs
Dogs can be taken on access land, but must be kept on leads of two metres or less between 1 March and 31 July, and at all times where they are near livestock. In addition land-owners may impose a ban on all dogs from fields where lambing takes place for up to six weeks in any year. Dogs may be banned from moorland used for grouse shooting and breeding for up to five years.

General Obstructions
Obstructions can sometimes cause a problem on a walk and the most common of these is where the path across a field has been ploughed over. It is legal for a farmer to plough up a path provided that it is restored within two weeks. This does not always

happen and you are faced with the dilemma of following the line of the path, even if this means treading on crops, or walking round the edge of the field. Although the latter course of action seems the most sensible, it does mean that you would be trespassing.

Other obstructions can vary from overhanging vegetation to wire fences across the path, locked gates or even a cattle feeder on the path.

Use common sense. If you can get round the obstruction without causing damage, do so. Otherwise only remove as much of the obstruction as is necessary to secure passage.

If the right of way is blocked and cannot be followed, there is a long-standing view that in such circumstances there is a right to deviate, but this cannot wholly be relied on. Although it is accepted in law that highways (and that includes rights of way) are for the public service, and if the usual track is impassable, it is for the general good that people should be entitled to pass into another line. However, this should not be taken as indicating a right to deviate when-ever a way is impassable. If in doubt, retreat.

Report obstructions to the local authority and/or the Ramblers (see page 94).

Useful Organisations

Campaign to Protect Rural England
5-11 Lavington Street,
London, SE1 0NZ
Tel. 020 7981 2800
www.cpre.org.uk

Camping and Caravanning Club
Tel. 024 7647 5426 (site bookings)
www.campingandcaravanningclub.co.uk

English Heritage
The Engine House, Fire Fly Avenue,
Swindon, SN2 2EH
www.english-heritage.org.uk

Forestry England
West England Regional Office
Tel. 0300 067 4800
www.forestryengland.uk

National Trust
Membership and general enquiries
Tel. 0344 800 1895
www.nationaltrust.org.uk
Regional Office
Wiltshire and Dorset
Tel. 01747 873250

Natural England
Tel. 0300 060 3900
www.gov.uk/government/organisations/
natural-england

Ordnance Survey
03456 05 05 05 (Lo-call)
www.ordnancesurvey.co.uk

Ramblers
2nd Floor, Camelford House,87-90 Albert
Embankment, London SE1 7TW
Tel. 0207 339 8500
www.ramblers.org.uk

Visit Wiltshire
www.visitwiltshire.co.uk

Local tourist information offices:
Amesbury: 01980 622525
Bradford-on-Avon: 01225 865797
Calne: 01249 814000
Corsham: 01249 714660
Devizes: 01380 800400
Malmsbury: 01666 822143
Marlborough: 01672 512487
Melksham: 01225 707424
Salisbury: 01722 342860
Swindon: 01793 466454
Trowbridge: 01225 765072
Warminster: 01985 218548
Westbury: 01373 825784

Traveline: 0871 200 2233

Youth Hostels Association
Trevelyan House, Dimple Road,
Matlock, Derbyshire DE4 3YH
Tel. 01629 592700
www.yha.org.uk

 Ordnance Survey maps of Wiltshire

Wiltshire is covered by Ordnance Survey 1:50 000 (1¼ inches to 1 mile or 2cm to 1km) scale Landranger map sheets 172, 173, 174, 183 and 184. These all-purpose maps are packed with useful information compiled to help you explore the area. In addition, they show viewpoints, picnic sites, places of interest and caravan and camping sites, as well as other information likely to be of interest.

To examine the Wiltshire area in more detail, and especially if you are planning walks, we recommend the following Ordnance Survey Explorer maps at 1:25 000 (2½ inches to 1 mile or 4cm to 1km) scale:
118 (Shaftesbury & Cranborne Chase)
130 (Salisbury & Stonehenge)
131 (Romsey, Andover & Test Valley)
142 (Shepton Mallet & Mendip Hills East)
143 (Warminster & Trowbridge)
156 (Chippenham & Bradford-on-Avon)
157 (Marlborough & Savernake Forest)

Text:	Dennis and Jan Kelsall. Some Wiltshire walks reused from PF (21)
	Somerset, the Mendips and Wiltshire, now superseded
Photography:	Brian Conduit, Nick Channer, Kevin Freeborn, and
	Dennis and Jan Kelsall. Page 31, © Shutterstock/Ron Ellis
Editorial:	Ark Creative (UK) Ltd
Design:	Ark Creative (UK) Ltd

ISBN: 978-0-31909-200-2

While every care has been taken to ensure the accuracy of the route directions, the
publishers cannot accept responsibility for errors or omissions, or for changes in details
given. The countryside is not static: hedges and fences can be removed, stiles can be
replaced by gates, field boundaries can alter, footpaths can be rerouted and changes in
ownership can result in the closure or diversion of some concessionary paths. Also, paths
that are easy and pleasant for walking in fine conditions may become slippery, muddy and
difficult in wet weather, while stepping stones across rivers and streams may become
impassable.
   If you find an inaccuracy in either the text or maps, please contact Trotman Publishing
at the address below.

First published 2022 by Trotman Publishing.

Trotman Publishing, 19-21D Charles Street, Bath, BA1 1HX
www.pathfinderwalks.co.uk

Printed in India by Replika Press Pvt. Ltd. 1/22

A catalogue record for this book is available from the British Library.

Front cover: Westbury White Horse
Title page: Looking back on the ascent of Cold Kitchen Hill

Ordnance Survey

Pathfinder® Guides

Britain's best-loved walking guides

Scotland
Pathfinder Walks
3   ISLE OF SKYE
4   CAIRNGORMS
7   FORT WILLIAM & GLEN COE
19 DUMFRIES & GALLOWAY
23 LOCH LOMOND, THE TROSSACHS, & STIRLING
27 PERTHSHIRE, ANGUS & FIFE
30 LOCH NESS & INVERNESS
31 OBAN, MULL & KINTYRE
46 ABERDEEN & ROYAL DEESIDE
47 EDINBURGH, PENTLANDS & LOTHIANS
82 ORKNEY & SHETLAND (spring 2022)
83 NORTH COAST 500 & NORTHERN HIGHLANDS
    (spring 2022)

North of England
Pathfinder Walks
15 YORKSHIRE DALES
22 MORE LAKE DISTRICT
28 NORTH YORK MOORS
35 NORTHUMBERLAND & SCOTTISH BORDERS
39 DURHAM, NORTH PENNINES & TYNE AND WEAR
42 CHESHIRE
49 VALE OF YORK & YORKSHIRE WOLDS
53 LANCASHIRE
60 LAKE DISTRICT
63 PEAK DISTRICT
64 SOUTH PENNINES
71 THE HIGH FELLS OF LAKELAND
73 MORE PEAK DISTRICT

Short Walks
1   YORKSHIRE DALES
2   PEAK DISTRICT
3   LAKE DISTRICT
13 NORTH YORK MOORS

Wales
Pathfinder Walks
10 SNOWDONIA
18 BRECON BEACONS
34 PEMBROKESHIRE & CARMARTHENSHIRE
41 MID WALES
55 GOWER, SWANSEA & CARDIFF
78 ANGLESEY, LLEYN & SNOWDONIA
    (spring 2022)
79 DEE VALLEY, CLWYDIAN HILLS & NORTH
    EAST WALES (spring 2022)

Short Walks
14 SNOWDONIA
31 BRECON BEACONS

Heart of England
Pathfinder Walks
6   COTSWOLDS
20 SHERWOOD FOREST & THE EAST MIDLANDS
29 WYE VALLEY & FOREST OF DEAN
74 THE MALVERNS TO WARWICKSHIRE
80 SHROPSHIRE
81 STAFFORDSHIRE
84 BERKSHIRE, BUCKINGHAMSHIRE &
    OXFORDSHIRE (spring 2022)

Short Walks
4   COTSWOLDS
32 HEREFORDSHIRE & THE WYE VALLEY

East of England
Pathfinder Walks
44 ESSEX
45 NORFOLK
48 SUFFOLK
50 LINCOLNSHIRE & THE WOLDS
51 CAMBRIDGESHIRE & THE FENS

South West of England
Pathfinder Walks
1   SOUTH DEVON & DARTMOOR
5   CORNWALL
9   EXMOOR & THE QUANTOCKS
11 DORSET & THE JURASSIC COAST
26 DARTMOOR
68 NORTH & MID DEVON
69 SOUTH WEST ENGLAND'S COAST
76 SOMERSET & THE MENDIPS (spring 2022)
77 WILTSHIRE (spring 2022)

Short Walks
8   DARTMOOR
9   CORNWALL
21 EXMOOR
29 SOUTH DEVON

South East of England
Pathfinder Walks
8   KENT
12 NEW FOREST, HAMPSHIRE & SOUTH DOWNS
25 THAMES VALLEY & CHILTERNS
54 HERTFORDSHIRE & BEDFORDSHIRE
65 SURREY
66 SOUTH DOWNS NATIONAL PARK & WEST SUSSEX
67 SOUTH DOWNS NATIONAL PARK & EAST SUSSEX
72 THE HOME COUNTIES FROM LONDON BY TRAIN

Short Walks
23 NEW FOREST NATIONAL PARK
27 ISLE OF WIGHT

Practical Guide
75 NAVIGATION SKILLS FOR WALKERS

City Walks
LONDON
OXFORD
EDINBURGH